Follow Your Heart's
Vegetarian
Soup Cookbook

Follow Your Heart's
Vegetarian
Soup Cookbook

By
Janice Cook Migliaccio

Woodbridge Press / Santa Barbara, California

Illustrated by Donna Wright
Cover Design by Biesek Design
Cover Photograph by Betty Bennet

1992
Published and distributed by
Woodbridge Press Publishing Company
Post Office Box 6189
Santa Barbara, California 93160
Copyright © 1983 by F.Y.H., a California Partnership

Printed in the United States of America

Distributed simultaneously in the United States and Canada

Library of Congress Catalog-in-Publication Data:

Migliaccio, Janice Cook.
Follow Your Heart's vegetarian soup cookbook.
Includes index.
1. Soups. 2. Vegetarian cookery. I. Follow Your Heart Natural
Foods Restaurants (Firm) II. Title.
III. Title: Vegetarian soup cookbook.
TX757.M54 1983 641.8'13 82-21822

ISBN 0-88007-131-1

Dear Jan, We love you! Michael, Bob, Paul, and Spencer

Contents

The Soups

Acknowledgments

Each Follow Your Heart soup cook has contributed enormously to this book, both by adding his or her own recipes to the repertoire and by continuing Follow Your Heart's soup tradition and teaching it to others. Recipes are like stories, told by one generation to the next and often improved and embellished with age. I would like to thank particularly the Follow Your Heart soup cooks, in approximate order of their arrival at Follow Your Heart.

Caren Diem Innes, Michael Besancon, Bob Goldberg, Debbi Edgar Holden, Spencer Windbiel, Paul Lewin, Micki Besancon, Robin Lowe, Terry Shields, John Barnes, Rachel McFaden, Bonnie Chappell McKelligott, Brion Levitsky, Kathleen Maloney, Marsha Stamp, Sharon Carson, Sondra McCaffrey, Hedy Kelho, Paul Reid, Taryn Seidel, Kelly Keelan, Scott Sandoz, Mark Levitsky, Mark Ludmer, Erly Lawrence, Diane Harvey, Stephanie Brown, Kristine Molasky-McCallister, Kathy Holm, Jeff Blagus, Dan Traub, Laurie Gomez, Maureen Brown, Bill Holsclaw, and any others whose names I may have overlooked, but whose soups live on.

I wish to thank all of our Follow Your Heart customers who have so enthusiastically sampled our soups over the years, offering continual support, constructive criticism, and suggestions. Your many requests helped to inspire this book's writing.

A special thank you to you soup testers, who patiently tried the recipes and evaluated them for me.

To my parents, Carol and Douglas Cook: I've always loved to cook, and you always gave me the freedom and encouragement to experiment and to learn. Your interest in natural foods, and all those whole wheat bread sandwiches I "had to" eat, as a kid, have been an inspiration. Thank you for your love and support. And thank you, too, for editing advice and nutrition information.

My sisters, Pamela and Linda Cook, and many health-minded friends have helped to spark my vegetarian ways. Thank you for the inspiration and whole new world of cooking that opened itself to me.

To my editor, Paulette Wamego: Thank you for clarifying and showing me what "I really meant" to say. I am grateful that the manuscript fell under your discerning eyes.

Our publisher, Howard Weeks, has been most understanding and encouraging. I've always felt that the book arrived at the right place. Thank you.

Special thanks to Donna Wright for your delightful illustrations, and your attunement to our soups; to Jack and Susan Biesek and Biesek Design for our lovely cover, and much attention to the small details; to Betty Bennett for the heartfelt cover photo; and to John-Roger, with love.

To my husband, Dale: Writing this book was not always easy, but you believed I would finish it even when I doubted. I am very aware of and appreciate your loving, support, and encouragement.

To Michael, Bob, Spencer, and Paul: You have provided me with a golden opportunity, and extended to me lots of faith and support. I thank each of you with much appreciation and love.

—*Janice Cook Migliaccio*

About
Follow Your Heart

Follow Your Heart began in 1970 as a small vegetarian lunch counter tucked into the corner of a natural foods store (in Canoga Park, California). In 1973, Follow Your Heart grew to include the store as well. From its inception the store and restaurant have been a center for the vegetarian and natural foods community, drawing more and more people who come to learn about health, enjoy the friendly atmosphere, and sample the tasty food. The food has always been of high quality, fresh and delicious, appealing to both vegetarians and nonvegetarians. Our soups continue to be of special interest to our customers, since their full-bodied, unique flavors are obtained without the use of meat.

In 1976, Follow Your Heart expanded and moved to a much larger store just a few blocks away (ironically, a former meat market). It consists of a fifty-seat restaurant and a complete natural foods store. It offers a large produce section, cheese and deli section, packaged natural foods products, all kinds of fresh juices, bulk grains, beans, herbs and spices, vitamins and supplements, books, baked goods, and sundries. The atmosphere is a cross between a mini-supermarket and an old-fashioned grocery store, with employees dedicated to helpful, personal service.

The restaurant, in addition to serving several homemade soups each day, offers a variety of sandwiches, salads, entrees, desserts, and beverages.

In September 1982 Follow Your Heart opened a second store in Santa Barbara (without a restaurant).

Follow Your Heart has grown tremendously since I first began cooking there in 1975. Then there were a total of twelve employees. It now employs about 100 people, all vegetarians. Michael Besancon founded Follow Your Heart in 1970, and by 1973 Bob Goldberg, Paul Lewin, and Spencer Windbiel had all joined with him in partnership. Their individual commitments to vegetarianism, as well as their continuing desire to learn and to share with others their knowledge of food, health, nutrition, and the vegetarian diet, have been responsible for Follow Your Heart's growth and the support of the community.

Follow Your Heart has a wonderful tradition of vegetarian soups. Many of the most successful recipes were written down over the years, to be used by other soup cooks as guidelines.

There is a certain style of soupmaking that most of Follow Your Heart's soup cooks use. Each new soup cook is trained extensively by two or three already experienced cooks, learning first to prepare popular and well-established soup recipes. After the training period, new cooks are free to create new recipes, providing their soups are delicious, nutritious, and enjoyed by our customers. Perhaps a primary ingredient that makes Follow Your Heart soups so popular is the fun and creativity that go into their making.

Customers have often requested our recipes; this book is Follow Your Heart's response. We welcome comments about our cookbook. Please feel free to write to us:

> Follow Your Heart
> 21825 Sherman Way
> Canoga Park, California 91303
> Attention: Soup Cookbook

Introduction

What is soup? An exquisite mix of delicious flavors in a broth or somewhat liquid base—chowders, stews, purees, and consommés all come under the classification of soup. They can be appetizers, almost salads (like gazpacho), flavorful side dishes, hearty main dishes, and even desserts (as fruit soup). Some soups are traditional fare, basic recipes from a particular country or cuisine. Sometimes a soup can capture just the flavor or essence of a particular style of cooking in a nontraditional way. Enchilada Soup, for example, a Follow Your Heart classic, is not a traditional way to serve an enchilada, but the taste buds will recognize the familiar flavor.

Soupmaking is an art with many aspects. There are lots of ways to cut a cauliflower, and many ways to season a soup. There is really no "correct" way to prepare a soup—but there are ways that work, and ways that don't. When I evaluate a finished soup, I consider whether

1) the soup smells delicious and invites tasting
2) the soup looks beautiful—color combinations are interesting and the colors complement each other
3) the soup tastes enjoyable and complete—you don't want to add anything to it
4) the vegetables are cut attractively, in shapes that go well together and in sizes that are easy to eat
5) ingredients are cooked to perfection, and perfection depends on how you want the soup to come out, or how the recipe is designed to turn out

6) the texture of the soup, the thick and thin of it, is appealing.

Texture and consistency vary greatly from soup to soup. At times you may want chunky, barely done potatoes, and at other times you may dice them into miniscule pieces and cook them down to mush. However, certain vegetables require especially careful cooking—it is no fun to chomp down on a nearly raw broccoli flowerette in a soup; and overcooked broccoli's olive drab color, strong odor, and disintegrating texture are unpleasant. But when cooked until just tender and a bright green, broccoli tastes wonderful.

A soup's consistency should complement the vegetables contained in it. Even when a soup is thin and brothy, it must not be watery; and a soup can be appealingly thick, as a stew or chowder, and not remind one of porridge.

Creativity in soupmaking is as unlimited as the cook's wildest imaginings. A favorite food, person, or a festive occasion is enough to inspire a wonderful soup—such as Dear Aunt Lilly's Lima Bean. Popeye's Swee'pea with Olive Oyl is another. Bilbo's Underground Stew, inspired by J. R. R. Tolkien's hobbit, contains only vegetables that are grown under the ground. An inspired name is enough to spark any soup eater's appetite. Anticipation and pleasure increase when a soup is served attractively, which encompasses the atmosphere, the table, the serving bowls and spoons. Success is complete when the soup tastes delicious, too.

Note that your soup will be more successful if your theme or idea is clear before you start. First visualize the kind of soup you'd like to create. What vegetables do you see in it, and how are they cut? Are they cooked until still firm or soft? Is the broth thick or thin? What colors are in the soup? Choose your ingredients according to your picture. Remember to relax and enjoy making your soup—it can be a whole lot of fun.

Basic Principles of Soupmaking

Equipment

These few simple kitchen items will aid in successful soupmaking.

Soup or stock pot—I recommend a 6- to 8-quart pot. A 6-quart pot will be large enough for all of the recipes in this book, but the larger pot makes stirring easier and keeps the stove top cleaner. I prefer a stainless steel, enameled cast iron, or enameled steel pot. Cast iron that is un-enameled is not recommended, as iron is released during cooking and often changes both the color and flavor of food cooked in it. I prefer not to use aluminum cookware, as it reacts with certain foods and becomes pitted with age.

Wooden spoons—at least two, with long handles. These are for stirring, not tasting, because wood absorbs lots of flavors and it is difficult to get a clear taste from it.

Knives—these few knives suit all my cooking needs: a large Chinese cleaver or a French chef's knife, a paring knife, and a thin serrated knife, all stainless steel. Keep a knife sharpener on hand—good sharp knives are much safer to work with than dull knives.

Grater—one with various grating sizes. This is especially useful when adding cheese to soup or grating vegetables for a soup base.

Blender—a necessary piece of equipment at Follow Your Heart, especially for making creamy soups. Blenders also .may be used to blend vegetables into puree and to grind

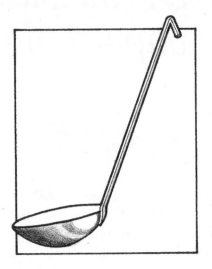

herbs—some have a 1-cup plastic container that is especially useful for this.

Soup ladle—6-ounce size, for serving.

Colander—a large one for washing and draining vegetables.

Herb grinder—an electric gadget that will turn large leafy dried herbs into a convenient powder (most will grind coffee beans, too). This gadget is unnecessary if your blender will grind herbs, or if you prefer to use a mortar and pestle.

Mortar and pestle—a simple hand tool for grinding herbs and spices into powder. Usually made of porcelain or wood, it consists of two pieces, a bowl or "mortar" in which to place the substance you are grinding, and a stick for grinding or pounding the substance, the "pestle." The

Japanese have a similar instrument known as a suribachi. It is a clay pot with a rough, unglazed inner surface, accompanied by a pestlelike wooden stick for grinding. Suribachis are available at natural food and Japanese food stores. Mortar and pestles can also be found at natural food stores, and in most cookware stores.

Garlic press—most Follow Your Heart soups contain some garlic, so I advise purchasing this simple timesaving device. It presses the garlic cloves into pieces smaller than most people would bother to cut them, which is an advantage. Try to press no more than a clove or two at a time, as too much pressure can easily break the common aluminum-alloy press. If you're lucky, you may be able to find a stainless steel press.

Seasonings

In the world of cooking, there is an unlimited supply of wonderful flavors to choose from: herbs, spices, and seasonings. They are unlimited in the sense that their different combinations are without end. It doesn't take long to get to know these delightful substances, just a little practice, experimentation, and experience.

The biggest mistakes in soupmaking usually involve overseasoning. You can always add a little more, but you cannot remove what's already there. Remember to keep soups simple in the first place. I speak from experience here, as I tend to see just how many flavors I can get into one recipe. The result is usually an uninteresting mishmash of flavors. Just a few seasonings at a time works best for me. If you like to use lots of flavors and that works for you, fine; but if you find that you can get carried away on a seasoning spree, just remind yourself that you don't have to use all seasonings at once—there will be other recipes to try them in.

It's important that the herbs and seasonings you choose complement your vegetables, rather than detract from or dominate them. Seasonings should praise the taste of a vegetable, rather than bury it. This takes practice and experience. Here's an easy way to learn: pour just a little

soup into a cup, add a little of the seasoning of your choice, and taste. When you find a combination you enjoy, add that to the whole soup in similar proportions.

Because all of Follow Your Heart's soups are vegetarian, people often wonder how we create our flavorful soup bases without using meat. One way is to use flavorful vegetables that are cooked long and well. Onions and celery, diced very fine and cooked from the soup's beginning, are essential ingredients in most Follow Your Heart soups. Near the start of a soup I also put in some of the heartier herbs that require long cooking time for best flavor, such as bay leaves, celery seed, rosemary, and thyme.

Any vegetable, if diced very small, or even grated, and

cooked for a long enough period to have a chance to break down, will contribute its unique flavor to soup broth. (If chunky bits of the same vegetable are desired in the soup, add these larger pieces toward the end of cooking.) For a sweet soup, try using yams, sweet potatoes, or carrots in the base, or a sweet winter or summer squash, or pumpkin. (A little carrot juice makes a sweet base too.) Use red or russet potatoes for a thick soup or chowder. Cabbage makes a slightly sweet and very tasty soup base too, and will even thicken a soup if you use enough of it. Split peas, lentils, and beans are flavorful, full-bodied additions.

Another way to add full flavor to a soup is to use a prepared seasoning product. These are usually added near the end of the soupmaking. Here are several we use often in our restaurant. These products are usually available at natural food stores.

Tamari (soy sauce, shoyu)—a traditional Oriental food, it is usually composed of soybeans, water, and salt, often with the addition of wheat, and is fermented and aged. It has a rich and delicious salty flavor. The soy sauces available in supermarkets are often made with chemicals that speed the aging process, and often contain sugar and preservatives. Natural food stores usually carry several good brands of traditionally made tamari, without unhealthful additives. Their flavor is also superior to that of the supermarket varieties—well worth the extra cost. I stress the importance of good tamari because we use it often in our recipes, and it is essential to the flavor of a good broth.

Tamari is also a delicious condiment to add to foods at the table. At my house we dilute tamari with water, half and half. People tend to use about the same amount of it whether it's full strength or diluted, and since it is quite salty, this little trick tends to keep salt intake down. However, recipes here call for full-strength tamari.

Dr. Bronner's "Balanced Protein-Seasoning"—made from soy; tasty in brothy vegetable soups. If unavailable in your area, substitute an equal amount of tamari, or to taste.

Naturade Instant Nutrition Drink, Vegetable Style—this tastes remarkably like chicken broth; great in noodle soups.

Bernard Jensen's Broth or Seasoning—lends itself well to creamy soups. It is also delicious as a dip when mixed into sour cream or yogurt. It is composed of barley, vegetables, seasonings and nutritional yeast, and does not contain salt. (If this product is not available where you live, look for a salt-free product with similar ingredients, such as Vegit, or salt-free vegetable bouillon cubes. The taste won't be exactly the same but will probably be close.

Spike Dee-licious Seasoning—a mixture of salt, seasonings, herbs, and spices. Spike has a unique, tangy flavor.

Vege-Sal—a mixture of salt and vegetable powders that may be used in recipes in place of salt.

About Salt

We use sea salt at Follow Your Heart rather than regular table salt. It is sun-dried ocean salt and contains trace minerals not found in regular salt, and is usually free of additives which may be found in table salt.

Any salt should be used with a light hand. At its best, salt helps to bring out other flavors and can add a complete taste to soups and other foods. A heavy touch, however, can dominate or obliterate more delicate flavors.

Salt needs vary a lot from person to person. Using salt sparingly in dishes prepared for others allows them to choose how salty they want their food.

Herbs and Spices

Herbs and spices are fragrant, subtle, sometimes mysterious additions to cooking. They can be the very essence of a soup's flavor, or they may simply add a little zest. They should always be used with care and considerable respect.

We use mostly dried herbs and spices at Follow Your Heart because they are more readily available than fresh, and easy to store. With prolonged storage, however, dried herbs lose their flavor, especially if ground or cut. It's best to use them within a year of purchase. If possible, buy

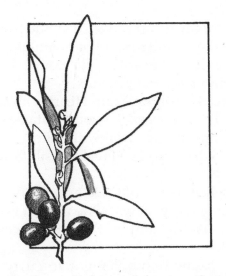

dried herbs in leaf or whole seed form rather than ground; they will retain their flavor much longer. Crumble leaves and grind seeds immediately before using (see "Equipment," for electric and hand methods of herb grinding).

Measure herbs carefully. Too much or too little can make a big difference in taste. For leaf herbs such as basil and oregano, measure herbs, then crumble the herb into the soup with your hands. Be aware that herbs and spices will not always have consistent freshness and flavor, and you, the cook, will need to adjust seasonings accordingly.

Many people display herbs and spices in shelves on a kitchen wall, often near a stove. Although this practice is attractive and convenient, exposure to light and heat greatly reduces the freshness of herbs and spices. Preserve their flavor by storing them in a cool, dark place.

I greatly enjoy growing fresh herbs at home. They take a minimum of space, many can be grown indoors or out, the plants are delightful to look at and to smell, and their fresh taste is incomparable. If you experiment with fresh herbs, you'll find that you need a larger quantity of fresh than dried, and fresh herbs may taste very different from their dried versions.

Allspice—actually ground from a single berry, this sweet spice tastes like a mixture of cinnamon, nutmeg, and clove. We use it in Pumpkin Pie Soup. Try it in soups containing winter squash or yams.

Basil—probably Follow Your Heart's favorite herb; we use it often. It is especially good in Italian and tomato-based soups, and it goes well with many vegetables. The herb is somewhat sweet. Fresh basil tastes incredibly good.

Bay leaf—delicious in split pea and bean soups, vegetable soups, and savory stews. One or two leaves per large pot of soup is usually ample. Remove leaves before serving.

Cardamom—a good complement to curry-type seasonings, it is strong, refreshing, and somewhat sweet. Use in small quantities.

Cayenne (red pepper)—spicy and hot, a little goes far, although different varieties vary in hotness. I use this instead of black pepper in most recipes. Cayenne is a stimulant, whereas many nutrition authorities consider black pepper an irritant.

Celery seed—an intense yet refreshing taste. Use small amounts, as this flavor is dominating. Use whole seed for long cooking periods (1 hour at least), ground seed for shorter cooking periods or close to the end of cooking.

Chili powder—should be fresh and fragrant. Chili powders vary greatly. It is the classic seasoning in chili soups or stews, but may be used to advantage in vegetable soups as well. Great sprinkled on popcorn.

Cilantro (coriander)—we use the fresh leaves in Mexican and East Indian soups especially. It has a strong, unusual flavor. The ground dried seeds are more commonly called for in recipes than are fresh leaves; they are also a main ingredient in curry powder. Look for fresh cilantro in Mexican or Indian grocery stores or in supermarkets with a Mexican produce section.

Cinnamon—ordinarily a dessert spice, this can also be used in savory soups. Try it with pumpkin and squash, split peas and lentils, and curried soups, in small amounts.

Cloves—can be used with the same types of soups as cinnamon, only be sure to use less of it. It is very strong and acquires an almost antiseptic taste when too much is used. Try just a pinch.

Cumin—naturally compatible with Mexican and Indian soups. Good in brothy vegetable soups, as well as in chili, split pea and bean soups.

Curry—a colorful mixture of flavorful spices, curry powders vary from brand to brand. Choose one with a good flavor that is not *too* hot. Curry lends itself well to such grains as rice and millet, and also goes well with lentils, split peas, and vegetables.

Dill seed and dill weed—both dill seed and dill weed are fragrant herbs, especially delicious in creamy potato-based or onion soups. The seed has a strong flavor and is best ground, used early in the cooking process so it will have a chance to blend. Dill weed, the leaf portion of the plant, is better added near the end of cooking to retain its best flavor and color.

Garlic—there are those people who do not particularly relish the taste of this flavorful plant. In small amounts it can add flavor without overrepresenting itself. At Follow Your Heart we like its taste and we use garlic often. Keep in mind the people you are cooking for as a gauge for its use.

Because we make soups at Follow Your Heart in quite large amounts, we usually use granulated garlic rather than fresh. It's much faster to use and easier to measure accurately, and so produces a more predictable flavor. The recipes in this book, with a few exceptions, have been converted to use fresh garlic. Fresh garlic tastes different from granulated and powdered, and a few recipes seemed to need the addition of the granulated and powdered garlics to achieve their classic taste. When using fresh garlic, I recommend a garlic press (see "Equipment" section).

Granulated garlic is a lot stronger than powdered, so use it accordingly. Granulated garlic dissolves into soups more easily than powdered. Both need to cook for at least a few minutes before serving, to dissolve fully and to assure well-blended flavors. When using granulated or powdered garlic, be sure the taste and smell is fresh. Old granulated or powdered garlic may become rancid and can spoil the flavor of good food.

Ginger—a wonderful, spicy root, used mostly in desserts and Oriental foods. The fresh root is often available in supermarkets. To prepare, thinly slice pieces of fresh ginger and add them to simmering soup—the longer they simmer, the more flavor. Remove before serving (they are quite spicy to the bite!). Another method is to finely grate fresh ginger. (I have seen special bamboo ginger graters for this purpose, but a fine metal grater will do.) Take the grated ginger and gently and tightly squeeze it with your clean hands, or press grated ginger in a garlic press, letting the juice run into a bowl. Add the juice to soup to taste. Discard pulp.

Powdered ginger may also be used. It's a strong spice, so start with small amounts.

Nutmeg—often used in desserts, it's quite good in soup too. Try it with spicy pumpkin and squash, and add just a dash to creamy vegetable soups, especially those containing spinach or mushroom.

Onion—scarcely a soup is made at Follow Your Heart without onion. Best flavor is attained when fresh onion are simmered into the soup at its beginning. We use mostly the yellow variety—it has a pleasant, mild, somewhat sweet flavor when cooked. Try white and red onions too for different flavors. Green onions are especially tasty, and attractive when thinly sliced and added to soups (miso soup is an example) just before serving. Leeks, with their mild, wonderful flavor, are another member of the onion family. Try them in Creamy Potato Leek Soup. Leeks need careful washing to rid them of sand (see "Washing, Soaking, and Cleaning" section).

We sometimes use onion powder and granulated onion. Fresh is preferable, but these work well enough if you're in a hurry or need to add onion flavor at the last minute. Granulated onion tastes especially good in creamy soups.

Oregano—this well-known herb can be used in a variety of ways. It's classic in Italian food. We use it often as a main flavoring ingredient in simple vegetable soups. It can produce a bitter taste when used in too large a quantity or when simmered too long. We almost always use leaf rather than ground oregano, finely crumbled into soups, and usually added toward the end of cooking. Oregano goes especially well with tomatoes, zucchini, and eggplant, and is great in bean and lentil soups. It is often teamed with basil, with excellent result.

Parsley—an emerald green jewel of an herb, parsley has a clean, refreshing taste. Try it finely minced in clear, brothy soups, in split pea soups, or in Cream of Green Things. It's great in salads, and makes an attractive garnish. Parsley stems can be a little tough or stringy, but they can be used when very finely chopped. A good knife or cleaver is a valuable tool here. Parsley has a reputation for freshening the breath, and is therefore an excellent complement to foods containing garlic and onions.

Rosemary—strong and aromatic, it is delightful in small

amounts. Try a pinch of ground rosemary in split pea and green vegetable soups. Too much of this one can be disastrous, dominating and antiseptic-tasting. If you use whole leaf rosemary, place it in a bag or tea ball to be removed before serving.

Tarragon—characterized by its distinctive sweet aroma, it is especially good in sweet-based soups like cream of carrot or sweet potato. It also tastes delicious in salad dressings.

Thyme—because it is often used as a seasoning for poultry, the flavor of thyme even when used in vegetarian dishes reminds me of stuffings and winter holiday meals. It is good with rice, split peas, and simple vegetable soups. Excessive amounts can result in a bitter flavor, so use moderation.

Special Food Items

The following ingredients are usually available in natural food stores. (See also "Seasonings" and "Herbs and Spices" sections.)

Bakon bits—vegetarian soy bits with a smoky, bacon flavor. Good substitute in recipes calling for bacon or ham.

Bakon yeast—in powder form, this is a smoked nutritional yeast product, used to produce a bacon or ham flavor. Use sparingly.

Miso—a centuries old, traditional Oriental food, miso is a paste made from fermented soybeans, sometimes containing other ingredients such as rice. It has a rich flavor and is rather salty, somewhat similar to tamari. It is usually added at the end of soupmaking, when the broth is still hot, but it should not be boiled. (Cooking destroys the enzymes and favorable bacteria it may have.)

Oils—look for cold-pressed oils. They have not under-gone high-heat processing, as have many commercial oils, and are free of preservatives and additives. Refrigerate after opening. Unrefined olive oil is quite flavorful and is sometimes recommended in these recipes. Cold-pressed and virgin olive oil are equivalent.

Potato flour—a powder made from dehydrated potatoes. It can be mixed with liquid in a blender and used as a thickening agent in soups (see "The Great Soup Rescue" section).

Raw dairy products—Follow Your Heart uses certified raw dairy products whenever possible. They contain en-zymes and nutrients which are destroyed during pasteuri-zation. Because they are not pasteurized, they have a shorter shelf life. I also think they have a fresher, superior flavor.

Textured vegetable protein—these plain or seasoned soy bits or chunks can be used in soups and stews, sloppy joe's, veggie burgers, etc.; sometimes referred to as TVP, a trademark of Archer Daniel Midland Company.

Wheat berries—for soups, red or winter wheat berries are

best: they have a chewier texture and stronger flavor than soft or spring wheat berries, which are good for making pastry flour. Wheat berries need ample soaking and cooking.

Yeast, nutritional—a specially grown food yeast, high in B vitamins and protein. It has a golden color and a pleasant, somewhat cheeselike flavor and is good added to soups, sauces, gravies, and popcorn.

Washing, Soaking, and Cleaning

There is nothing quite like biting into gritty spinach. Joyful anticipation of the next delicious bite is turned suddenly to fearful expectation.

Some vegetables require special cleaning to increase their palatability. Spinach and leeks are two vegetables which need thorough washing before other preparation can take place. You may find these methods effective for some other dirty vegetables as well.

Spinach (or Other Leafy Greens): The Two Soak, Two Rinse Method

Cut off roots and base of stems and discard. Place leaves in a sink or large bowl filled with cool water, and swish them around to remove dirt. Let sit for *no more than 5 minutes* (this helps to loosen remaining dirt). Excess soaking of spinach can cause soggy, wilted leaves, so watch time carefully. Remove leaves to a large colander, and drain and clean wash basin thoroughly. Rinse leaves under cool running water, stirring them gently so water reaches all leaves.

Repeat soaking procedure. Repeat rinsing procedure. Drain thoroughly. Your spinach should be sparkling clean, all grit removed.

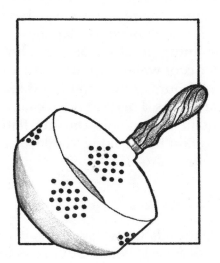

Leeks

Dirt likes to hide in the inner leaves, so thorough washing of this delectable member of the onion family is required. Here's the best way I've found to clean a leek. Remove root ends and thinly slice leek into rounds (I use most of the green part as well, except parts that look dry or wilted). Place leek slices in a colander, and rinse under cool water, stirring with your hands, until all soil is rinsed away. Drain.

The one disadvantage to this method is that some fragrant leek juice is lost in washing. So, wash leeks quickly to retain most of their flavor.

Beans

Beans usually require careful picking over before they are ready to even soak. Small rocks or tiny clumps of dirt, the same size as the beans, are often present.

Before measuring, spread your beans out on a counter so you can see them. Pick out and discard rocks, dirt, or any other foreign matter. Remove beans that look shriveled, discolored, spoiled, or damaged, and discard.

Measure remaining good beans according to your recipe. Rinse under cool water to remove dust and dirt. Soak beans for several hours or overnight in three to four times more water than beans. I discard the soaking water, as it is reputed to contain ingredients causing flatulence. There are those who retain the soaking water for cooking, however, so choose for yourself.

Insect-Infested Produce

If you buy organically grown produce, it's a good idea to check carefully for insects before buying. A bug or two can be rinsed off or removed and does no harm, but produce such as broccoli, cauliflower, and leafy lettuce sometimes harbors insects on inner surfaces. If you happen to find lots of bugs in your vegetables, try soaking vegetables in a sink full of cool water for a few minutes. Many bugs will float right off. Rinse.

Scrubbing versus Peeling

Valuable nutrients are often contained in the skin or just below the skin of vegetables and fruits, so we don't peel them. Scrub them just enough to remove dirt and wax. Commercial cucumbers are an exception. They are so waxy that they need their peel removed before eating. But hothouse varieties are available with edible skins.

The Great Soup Rescue

Even the best soupmakers sometimes find themselves in hot water. Here are some common problems, and some creative ways to deal with them. You may also discover some of your own.

Not all cooking mistakes are salvageable, but it's amazing how creative a cook can get in the face of adversity. One of our best cooks, Mark Levitsky, badly burned a tomato lentil soup. General opinion was that the soup was a candidate for the garbage disposal. But Mark persevered, adding one seasoning and then another, until he created a wonderful soup called Hickory-Smoked Lentil. (The name added greatly to the attractiveness of this soup.) It really did taste good—several customers called later to request the recipe. We were rather embarrassed to say there was none. And no recipe is included in this volume, either.

Lack of attention is probably the most common cause of cooking errors, especially in soupmaking. If you are following a recipe, read through it first so you understand its timing and the terms used. This will help avoid unpleasant surprises. If you don't understand a cooking term, look it up in a reputable cookbook.

Give yourself plenty of undistracted time to prepare a recipe, especially the first time you try it. Use a timer if necessary. Instructions like "stir occasionally," or "heat at lowest setting," may prevent burns and should be carefully followed. *Use the recipe to your advantage.*

If you are an inexperienced cook, I recommend following recipes at first, until you feel competent and confident enough to create your own. Ask someone whose cooking you enjoy to recommend good beginning cookbooks that won't overwhelm you with complex techniques and unusual ingredients. Choose recipes that look simple and are easy for you to understand. The best-tasting recipes are often the simplest, anyway.

Sometimes overconfidence causes cooking errors—the cook may add too much of an ingredient without bothering to add it gradually and to taste. Sometimes the cook knows a recipe by heart, becomes casual about it, and doesn't give it proper attention. It's humbling to ruin a favorite recipe you've made many times before.

Faulty recipes: it's a fact that some cookbooks make it into print with inadequate directions or with recipes that have not been thoroughly tested. Sometimes it's the cookbook, not the cook, that is at fault. If you have poor results from one cookbook, find another.

Burned Soup

At the first sign of a burned soup (a tell-tale aroma is revealing), turn off heat. Pour the burned soup carefully into another pot, being careful not to scrape the burned bottom. Sometimes this quick action is all that's necessary to save a soup.

If the transferred soup still smells burned, taste it. Sometimes you can smell the burn, but it still tastes fine. If it tastes burned also, consider adding seasonings that will help mask the flavor. Salt and tamari can help. Or consider going to a barbecued taste, as our cook Mark did with Hickory-Smoked Lentil. Does the soup lend itself to the addition of tomato sauce and chili seasonings?

A mild flavored soup, when burned, is eternally altered, although possibly salvageable. Sometimes the addition of potatoes will help to absorb a burned flavor, but you'll probably need to cook them first, at least partially, or grate them so they'll cook quickly. When a delicate or mild tasting soup is burned, you'll likely have to abandon delicacy and add herbs and seasonings that will mask the burned flavor.

A soup that's already burned once will usually burn again easily, so very low heat and frequent stirring is recommended if you must continue cooking.

Burns are usually caused by lack of water; heavy or starchy ingredients, cooked improperly (such as beans, macaroni, and potatoes, which have a tendency to sink to the bottom of the pot); cooking thick soups too long or on too high heat; inadequate stirring; scorching of cheese or milk products on high heat.

A frequent cause of burns is "breaking the boil." If ingredients are added to a simmering soup too quickly or in too large amounts, the cool ingredients may cool the soup enough to break the boil. The new ingredients tend to sink to the bottom and can easily burn. This especially occurs in thick soups. Once a soup such as bean or split pea has begun to thicken, add ingredients carefully.

Adding dairy products can make a burned taste less intense. But if a soup is burned too badly, throw it out rather than adding lots of ingredients in an attempt to save it. No use throwing good ingredients after bad. Sometimes it's better to start over. Try to figure out what went wrong, of course, so you can make the soup successfully next time. It's a great feeling of confidence to complete a recipe beautifully the second or third time, when it was not so great on the first try.

Over-Salting

The best way to prevent over-salting is to taste salty ingredients before they go into the pot. Plain old sea salt is not the only offender: be watchful of prepared seasonings which contain salt, like tamari, Spike, celery salt, etc. Cheese can also be very salty, as can nutritional yeast and bakon flavorings (see "Special Food Items" section). Prepared tomato sauces are often very salty too. If you use these ingredients, you may want to reduce or eliminate added salt in a recipe.

If you do over-salt, there are ways to compensate. Potatoes can again save the day: they are wonders at absorbing salty flavor. Mashed potatoes work well too (provided they are unsalted). You can also use potato flour (listed under "Special Food Items"). Blend it with water or soup broth in a blender until smooth, then add to soup (this prevents lumps from forming). Rice or other plain cooked grains will also help absorb salt.

The addition of unsalty dairy products such as milk, cream, or sour cream can also help reduce saltiness. Consider enlarging salty soups. Adding more water may be all that's necessary, although that may require adding more vegetables and other seasonings as well.

Over-Seasoning

A too strong herb flavor, such as too much rosemary or oregano, can make a soup very unpleasant, even bitter. The best way to handle this is to stretch the soup with water, milk, or cream. Potatoes or grains may help absorb strong flavors. Sometimes the addition of other seasonings can help mask flavors, but you'd better know your seasonings before you try this, or things may just get worse. Enlarging the soup until the offending herb or seasoning becomes a background flavor is your best bet.

Miscellaneous Tips and Suggestions

Cutting Vegetables

The way you choose to cut vegetables will greatly affect the look, taste, and the eating-ease of your soup.

The recipes in this book often specify how a vegetable should be cut. This is probably the way the person who invented the soup cut his or her vegetables, and I've kept with tradition in most cases. This gives you a more authentic Follow Your Heart soup. However you decide to cut your veggies, keep in mind that 1) they should be attractive, and easy to gather onto a spoon and to spoon into a mouth; 2) the different cuts of vegetables should look well with each other; and 3) they should be cut to achieve a desired result, for example, finely diced to dissolve into a base, or cut in larger chunks to remain somewhat firm and intact.

This is also a way to put your personal, creative stamp on your soup. I've sometimes guessed a soup's creator just from the shape and size of the vegetables.

Children's Vegetable Soup

Use a basic soup like Rainbow Vegetable or Old Fashioned Stew (or any soup kids will like). Cut the vegetables in smaller, kid-size pieces and fun shapes—circles, squares, triangles, etc. You may need to reduce the soup's cooking time in some instances, as the smaller pieces of vegetables will cook more quickly. Also, whole wheat alphabet noodles, as well as spiral, shell, and elbow-shaped pastas that children especially enjoy, are sometimes available.

Dairy Products

They should never be boiled or added to too-hot soup, as they will toughen and scorch. Always add them near the end of soupmaking. Butter is the exception. Since it is almost all fat, it can go into a soup right at the beginning. (The protein in other dairy products is the part that toughens and curdles.)

Reheating and Freezing Soups

In the restaurant, soups are made in 40-quart batches. I've reduced recipes here to 3-5 quarts. That's still quite a bit of soup. However, soups can be refrigerated for a few days and reheated, and in most cases the flavor seems to improve with a couple of days' aging. Just be careful when reheating not to boil soups containing dairy products, as they will curdle when boiled (butter is an exception). Simply simmer gently until hot. Most of the soups will freeze quite well also, though their colors and textures may change somewhat and freezing does harm some vitamins.

Creating Your Own Soups

Using the recipes in this book as a guide, you can try your own creative hand at soupmaking. If you want to make a type of bean soup not covered here, for example, look for a recipe that calls for a similar type of bean and follow approximate cooking procedures and times (of course, you may want to use entirely different seasonings).

People love soups, and for good reason. They can be satisfying, heart- and stomach-warming, nourishing and delicious, and they allow for endless creativity and discovery in cooking.

The Soups

Although none of these soups is really difficult to make, some are simpler and quicker than others. Approximate preparation time (not including time for soaking beans or grains) is given for each soup and easy soups are noted.

Au Gratin Potato Soup

Bob Goldberg

Easy
Cooking time: 50 min.   Makes 4 qts.

Thick and cheesy, delicious with a crisp green salad.

8 c. water
6 lg. russet potatoes (unpeeled)—
    4 diced; 2 quartered
    lengthwise, then sliced $\frac{1}{4}''$ thick
4 Tbsp. butter
1 c. thinly sliced green onions
1 Tbsp. Jensen's broth powder

1 tsp. granulated garlic
1 tsp. bakon flavored yeast, or
    $\frac{1}{2}$ tsp. bakon bits
$\frac{3}{4}$ lb. sharp Cheddar, grated (3 c.
    packed)
1–2 tsp. paprika

Place water, diced potatoes, and butter together in a 5- or 6-quart pot. Bring to a boil, then cook, covered, over medium heat for 20–30 minutes, or until potatoes begin to break down and a thick broth forms.

Lower heat to simmer and add sliced potatoes. Simmer, covered, about 10 minutes, until potatoes are barely tender.

Add green onions, Jensen's broth powder, and garlic. Remove from heat.

In blender, blend until smooth: bakon yeast or bits, grated Cheddar, and $1\frac{1}{2}$ cups of the hot soup broth. (Try to avoid using potato chunks for this.) Add blended mixture back to soup in pot, and place soup over low heat, stirring occasionally, until hot but not boiling. This should take only a few minutes. Stir in paprika, to desired color—it is very mild tasting. Serve.

Baked Potato Soup

Bob Goldberg

Cooking time: 1 hr.   Makes 4½ qts.

The hearty taste of baked potatoes with sour cream and chives. (Cooking time does not include baking of potatoes.)

5 lg. russet potatoes, baked—	1 Tbsp. Spike
3 diced; 2 cut into lg. chunks	1 tsp. bakon flavored yeast or
4 c. diced yellow onion	1 Tbsp. bakon bits
¼ c. butter	1 c. sour cream
8 c. water	1 3-oz. pkg. cream cheese,
1 c. diced green onion	softened
1 tsp. garlic powder	1 c. milk
2 Tbsp. Jensen's broth powder	¼ lb. mild Cheddar cheese,
½ tsp. sea salt	shredded
¼ c. dried chives	

Bake all 5 potatoes at 425° for 40 minutes to 1 hour, depending on size. Test for doneness with a fork. Cool potatoes until firm, at least 2 hours.

Dice three of the baked potatoes (about 6 cups) and bring to a boil with yellow onions, butter, and water. Lower heat to simmer, and cook, covered, stirring occasionally, until potatoes begin to break down.

When a thick broth forms, turn off heat and add remaining 2 potatoes, cut into large chunks (about 4 cups). Add green onions, garlic powder, Jensen's broth powder, salt, chives, and Spike. (The heat is turned off while preparing the dairy ingredients so that potato chunks don't break down.)

In blender, blend bakon flavored yeast or bakon bits with 1 cup soup broth until thoroughly blended (bakon bits should be dissolved). Add to soup. Then combine in blender: sour cream, cream cheese, milk, and grated

Cheddar. Blend until smooth. Add to soup. Return soup
to heat and simmer, gently, until hot but not boiling, stirring constantly. Adjust seasonings to taste. Garnish with
chopped chives, green onions, or sprigs of fresh parsley, if
desired.

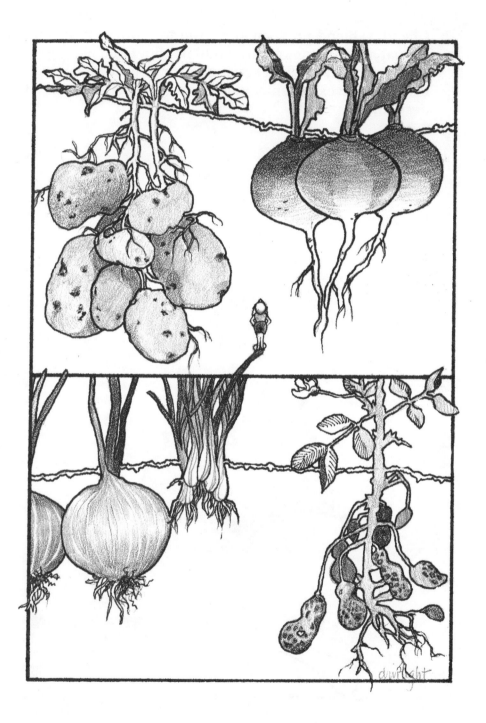

Bilbo's Underground Stew

Bob Goldberg

Cooking time: $1\frac{1}{4}$ hrs.   Makes $4\frac{1}{2}$ qts.

Inspired by the famous hobbit, all of the vegetables in this soup are grown underground. It has an unusual earthy flavor and a bright pink color, from the beets.

8 c. water
1 c. raw, blanched Virginia peanuts (or other raw or roasted peanuts, no skins)
3 c. turnips, chopped into bite-sized chunks
1 c. diced red onion
1 c. diced yellow onion
2 c. russet potatoes, cut in large chunks
2 c. carrots, sliced in $\frac{1}{4}$" rounds
$1\frac{1}{2}$ c. rutabaga, parsnip, jicama, or Jerusalem artichoke, or any combination of these

1 c . beets (unpeeled, well-scrubbed), cut in small chunks
1 c. sliced green onion (bulb and tops)
2 c. water
1 Tbsp. granulated garlic
1 Tbsp. dried parsley, crumbled
1 Tbsp. dried basil, crumbled
1 Tbsp. Spike
2 Tbsp. tamari
$\frac{1}{4}$ c. dried chives
4 Tbsp. ($\frac{1}{2}$ cube) butter
2 c. (1 pt.) sour cream

Bring to a boil: water, peanuts, turnips, and red and yellow onion. Simmer, covered, stirring occasionally until vegetables break down and a slightly thickened broth forms, about 45 minutes. Add potatoes, carrots, rutabaga (or alternate vegetable), and water. Bring to a boil again, then simmer, covered, stirring occasionally, until potatoes are barely tender. Add beets, green onions, garlic, parsley, basil, Spike, and tamari, and simmer until beets are just tender. Soup will be a bright pink. Turn off heat. Stir in chives, butter, and sour cream, and let sit, covered, 5 minutes. Stir well and serve.

Beet Borscht

Bob Goldberg

Easy
Cooking time: 35 min.   Makes 1½ qts.

A traditional soup, simple to prepare. Serve with pumper-nickel bread.

5 c. water
4 c. (6 med.) beets, peeled, cut in julienne strips
½ c. finely diced yellow onion
2 tsp. safflower oil

1 Tbsp. apple cider vinegar, or to taste
1 tsp. Dr. Bronner's seasoning powder
sea salt to taste (optional)

In a tightly covered 3-quart pot, bring water, beets, and onion to a boil. Reduce heat and simmer, covered, about 15 minutes or until vegetables are quite tender.

Add oil, vinegar (amount depends on strength of vinegar—I used full strength), and Dr. Bronner's seasoning powder. Continue simmering about 10 minutes more.

Add sea salt and, if desired, additional water. Serve warm or chilled, topped with a dollop of sour cream and a sprinkling of dill weed or chives.

Broccoli Almond Soup

Sondra McCaffrey

Easy
Cooking time: 45 min.

Makes 3½ qts.

A simple to make soup, for broccoli lovers.

8 c. water
2 c. diced yellow onion
1¼ c. thinly sliced raw almonds or
  blanched whole raw al-
  monds—reserve ¼ c. for garnish
2 c. thinly sliced celery (including
  leaves)
2 lbs. broccoli—4 c. sliced stems;
  6 c. bite-sized flowerettes

½ c. tamari
3 lg. cloves garlic, pressed or
  minced
2 tsp. Spike
4 Tbsp. butter or margarine
1 Tbsp. crumbled oregano
1 tsp. crumbled basil

In a 4½- or 5-quart pot, bring to a boil: water, onion, 1 cup of the almonds, and celery. Simmer, covered, for 20 minutes, or until onions are tender.

Meanwhile prepare broccoli. Cut off and discard woody stems. Thinly slice remaining stems. (If stems are wide you may want to chop them into still smaller pieces.) Break flowerettes into very small, bite-sized pieces, and set aside for later. When onions are tender, add the chopped broccoli stems, tamari, garlic, Spike, butter, oregano, and basil. Simmer, covered, for 10 minutes.

Add reserved flowerettes, and simmer 5–10 minutes, or until flowerettes are barely tender and bright green. If a thinner soup is desired, add 1–2 cups water. Adjust seasonings to taste. Serve garnished with reserved almonds.

Broccoli Wheatberry

Sondra McCaffrey

Cooking time: 1½ hrs.   Makes 2½–3 qts.

A long soaking time is essential to tenderize the wheat berries. They give the soup an unusual, slightly nutty flavor and texture.

¾ c. whole red wheat berries, presoaked
9 c. water
2 Tbsp. unrefined olive oil
2 c. (2 med.) chopped yellow onion
1½ c. sliced celery
2 lbs. broccoli—4 c. sliced stems; 4 c. bite-sized flowerettes
5 Tbsp. tamari
4 tsp. Jensen's broth powder

3 med. cloves garlic, pressed or minced
2 tsp. crumbled basil leaf
1 10-oz. pkg. frozen peas, rinsed under hot water to thaw, or 2 c. shelled fresh peas, lightly steamed until tender and bright green
2 Tbsp. nutritional yeast flakes
¼ tsp. Vege-Sal

Soak wheat berries in 3 cups water for 12 hours. Drain; discard soaking water.

In a 5- or 6-quart pot, bring to a boil: 8 cups of the water, olive oil, presoaked wheat berries, onion, and celery. Reduce heat and simmer, covered, about 45 minutes, or until wheat berries are slightly tender.

To prepare broccoli, first discard woody stems. Cut or break flowerettes into bite-sized pieces, and set aside. Thinly slice remaining stems, to equal about 4 cups.

Add broccoli stems, tamari, Jensen's broth powder, garlic, and basil. Simmer, covered, about 25 minutes, or until wheat is tender (it will still have a slightly chewy quality).

Add flowerettes and the remaining 1 cup water, and simmer about 5 minutes.

Add peas, yeast, and Vege-Sal, stirring to dissolve yeast. Simmer a few minútes, or until broccoli tops are just tender and still a bright green. Adjust seasonings to taste. Serve.

Cheesy Tomato Spanish Rice

Hedy Kelho

Cooking time: 1 hr.   Makes 3½–4 qts.

A very tasty Spanish soup, popular with our customers.

2 c. water
¾ c. long grain brown rice,
  uncooked
2 c. (4 lg. stalks) finely chopped
  celery
1½ c. (2 med.) diced carrot
2 Tbsp. chili powder
8 c. tomato puree—4 lbs.
  chopped, unpeeled ripe
  tomatoes (or 3 1-lb. cans whole
  or diced tomatoes and 2 c. water) blended until smooth

4 oz. (½ c.) canned mild green
  chilies, diced
2½ tsp. ground cumin
½ tsp. granulated garlic
1 lg. fresh ripe tomato, chopped
  (optional)
¼ lb. grated mild Cheddar cheese
¼ lb. grated jack cheese
½ c. sour cream
¾ c. diced green onions
sea salt or tamari to taste
  (optional)

In a 5- or 6-quart pot, bring to a boil: water, rice, celery, carrots, and 1 tablespoon of the chili powder. Turn heat to low and simmer, covered tightly, for about ½ hour, or until rice is slightly tender. (Check once or twice to make sure there's enough cooking water—add a little if necessary.)

Add blended tomatoes and diced green chilies. Bring to a second boil. Reduce heat and continue simmering, covered, about 15 minutes, or until rice is quite tender. Stir occasionally.

Add remaining 1 tablespoon of chili powder, cumin, garlic, and fresh chopped tomato, and continue simmering about 10 minutes, or until flavors are well blended.

Turn burner to lowest heat. Add Cheddar and jack cheese, sour cream, and green onions, stirring quickly to blend well. Heat gently for 5 minutes (without boiling). Add salt or tamari to taste, if desired. Serve.

Cheezy Zucchini

Brion Levitsky

Easy
Cooking time: 1¼ hrs.   Makes 3 qts.

A great way to use the overflow of squash from a summer garden. This easy soup is one of our favorites.

6 c. water
3 c. diced yellow onion
3½ lbs. squash—5 c. (1½ lbs.) diced (may be a combination of zucchini, yellow squash, and summer squash, using at least half zucchini); 7 c. (2 lbs.) zucchini squash, sliced in thin half-rounds (if using very small zucchini, cut in thin rounds)

3–4 Tbsp. butter
2¼ tsp. crumbled oregano leaf
1½ tsp. granulated garlic
6 oz. grated sharp Cheddar cheese
3-oz. pkg. cream cheese
3 Tbsp. tamari
¼ tsp. black pepper, or tiny pinch of cayenne
sea salt or Vege-Sal to taste

To make stock, in a 5- or 6-quart pot bring to a boil: water, onion, diced squash, and butter. Cook, covered, over medium heat until squash begins to break down and form a broth—about 45 minutes to 1 hour.

Add sliced zucchini, oregano, and garlic, and bring to a boil again. Reduce heat to simmer, and continue cooking for 5–10 minutes, or until zucchini slices are slightly tender. Turn heat to lowest setting.

In a tightly covered blender container (it's hot!), blend together 1½ cups of the hot soup broth (including some of the zucchini slices) and the Cheddar and cream cheese until smooth. Add to soup.

Turn off heat; add tamari, pepper, and salt, to taste. Serve.

Chili-Style Lentil

Sondra McCaffrey

Cooking time: 1¼ hrs.   Makes 3½–4 qts.

A chili variation, and no beans to soak. Delicious served with corn bread.

6½ c. water
2½ c. (1 lb.) lentils, dry
1½ Tbsp. unrefined olive oil
2½ c. (2 med.) chopped yellow
  onion
2½ c. (2–3 lg. stalks) chopped
  celery
3 Tbsp. tamari
2 Tbsp. chili powder
1½ Tbsp. ground cumin
2 tsp. granulated garlic
2 tsp. granulated onion

2 tsp. crumbled basil leaf
1 8-oz. can Spanish-style tomato
  sauce
1 7-oz. can (or 2 4-oz. cans) mild
  green chilies, whole or diced
1 28-oz. can whole peeled
  tomatoes (including juice),
  chopped
1 Tbsp. Vege-Sal, or 2 tsp. sea
  salt, or to taste
½ tsp. (or less) cayenne pepper
  (optional—some like it hot)

In a 5- or 6-quart pot with a tight-fitting lid, bring to a boil: water, lentils, olive oil, chopped onion, and celery. Simmer, covered, about 35 minutes, or until lentils are a little tender.

Add tamari, chili powder, cumin, garlic, granulated onion, and basil. Continue simmering until lentils are quite tender, about 20 minutes. Stir occasionally.

In a blender, blend tomato sauce with green chilies until smooth. (No need to remove seeds from chilies.) Add to soup, along with the chopped canned tomatoes and their juice. Stirring often, simmer for 15 minutes or until flavors are well blended. Add Vege-Sal or sea salt, and cayenne if desired. Soup should be of medium thickness; add water if necessary. Adjust seasonings to taste. Serve.

Coconut Curried Rice

Robin Lowe

Cooking time: 1 hr.   Makes 2½–3 qts.

An exotic, East Indian–style soup with a fruity, spicy flavor.

2½ Tbsp. olive oil
7 tsp. (2⅓ Tbsp.) curry powder
2 tsp. paprika
¾ c. long grain brown rice, uncooked
5 c. water
1½ c. chopped yellow onion
3 c. chopped celery
¾ c. carrot, sliced in ¼″ rounds
1¼ tsp. granulated garlic
5 Tbsp. tamari
1¼ c. unsweetened long thread
  coconut

1 10-oz. pkg. frozen peas, rinsed
  under hot water to thaw, or 2
  c. shelled fresh peas, lightly
  steamed until tender and
  bright green
1½ c. pineapple juice
½ c. Barbados or other light
  molasses (not blackstrap!)
sea salt to taste
1½–2 c. plain yogurt (optional)

In a heavy-bottomed 5-quart pot, gently heat olive oil. Add 4 teaspoons of the curry powder, paprika, and rice. Heat over a very low flame for about 10 minutes, stirring frequently, until the mixture has a pleasant roasted smell and seasonings are a deep brown color. (If seasonings turn black, however, and it smells burned, you'll have to discard and start over.)

Add water, onion, celery, and carrot, and bring to a rolling boil. Simmer, covered, for about 20 minutes, or until rice is a little tender. Add garlic, the remaining 1 tablespoon (3 teaspoons) curry powder, and tamari, and continue simmering about 20 minutes longer, or until rice is fully cooked.

Add coconut, peas, pineapple juice, molasses, and salt to taste. Stir in yogurt (optional) and heat gently until thoroughly hot, but not boiling. Adjust seasonings if necessary. Serve.

Chilled Summer Fruit Soup

Dan Traub

Easy
Cooking time: $\frac{1}{2}$ hr.   Makes $3\frac{1}{2}$ qts.

Cool and refreshing, this makes an excellent first course or dessert.

1 lb. pitted sweet cherries
1 lb. seedless green grapes
$\frac{3}{4}$ lb. diced pippin apples
  (unpeeled)
2 c. water
$\frac{3}{4}$ c. concord grape juice
$\frac{1}{2}$ c. pineapple juice
$\frac{1}{4}$ c. red wine
$\frac{1}{2}$ tsp. grated orange rind
$\frac{1}{4}$ lb. pitted prunes, diced
  ($\frac{1}{2}$ c. packed)
1 pt. berries—whole blueberries,
  raspberries, or boysenberries,
  or halved strawberries

4 tsp. arrowroot or kuzu powder
  (crush with rolling pin if
  lumpy)
2 Tbsp. fruit juice (or water)
3–4 Tbsp. maple syrup or honey,
  or to taste
$\frac{3}{4}$ lb. seedless oranges, peeled and
  thinly sliced
plain yogurt or sour cream, as
  topping (optional)
sprigs of fresh mint, and/or fresh
  uncooked berries or cherries,
  as garnish

In a 5- or 6-quart pot, combine cherries, grapes, apples, water, grape juice, pineapple juice, wine, and orange rind. Bring to a boil. Reduce heat, cover and simmer about 10 minutes, or until apples are just tender. Stir occasionally.

Add prunes and berries. Continue simmering, about 5 minutes, or until prunes are tender.

Mix arrowroot with the 2 tablespoons water or fruit juice until completely dissolved. Add to soup, stirring quickly to blend, and bring soup to a boil. Stir constantly while boiling for 1 minute. Remove from heat.

Add maple syrup or honey, and orange slices. Chill.

Serve topped with yogurt or sour cream, if desired, and garnished with mint leaves and fruit.

Note: This soup is equally delicious served warm.

Corn Chowder

Bob Goldberg
Paul Lewin
Marsha Stamp

Cooking time: 1 hr.   Makes 4½ qts.

A favorite soup, this is thick, rich and delicious. The cauliflower, when cooked to the right consistency, almost resembles pieces of clam. A variation of this recipe may be made without dairy products.

5 c. water
6 c. russet potato
  (unpeeled)—3 c. diced; 3 c.
  chopped into fairly large
  chunks
2 c. diced yellow onion
5 c. corn, fresh or frozen (if
  frozen, rinse under hot water
  to thaw, then measure)
1½ c. thinly sliced celery
1½ c. finely diced green cabbage
1 lg. head (1 lb.) cauliflower—
  ¾ c. diced core; 2½–3c. bite-
  sized flowerettes

4 Tbsp. butter
2 tsp. basil
¼ c. minced fresh parsley
2 Tbsp. Spike
2 tsp. granulated garlic
1 tsp. dill weed
1 c. sour cream
1 c. cream cheese
½ c. milk
3 Tbsp. nutritional yeast flakes
2 Tbsp. dried chives
sea salt, or more Spike, to taste

To prepare cauliflower, discard woody portion of stem, then slice cauliflower into quarters. Cut the center core from the flowerettes. Finely dice the core pieces (and any leaves) to equal about $\frac{3}{4}$ cup. Break the flowerettes into small pieces and reserve for later.

In a 5- or 6-quart pot, prepare soup stock by bringing to a boil: water, diced potatoes, onion, $1\frac{1}{2}$ cups of the corn, celery, cabbage, diced cauliflower core, butter, and basil. Cook, covered, over low heat until potatoes begin to dissolve, about $\frac{1}{2}$ hour. Stir occasionally.

Meanwhile, prepare the remaining $3\frac{1}{2}$ cups corn, chopped potatoes, parsley, Spike, garlic, and dill weed so you'll be able to add them all at once. Add these ingredients when the potatoes in the stock begin to break down. Simmer, covered, about 10 minutes, stirring occasionally.

Add reserved cauliflowerettes and continue cooking another 10 minutes, or until potato chunks are tender but still intact, and cauliflowerettes are a little tender but still chewy. When vegetables reach these stages, turn burner to lowest heat.

In blender, blend together sour cream, cream cheese, and milk until smooth. Add to soup, along with nutritional yeast and chives. Heat gently without boiling. Add Spike or sea salt to taste. When hot, serve, garnished with sprigs of fresh parsley if desired.

Note: For this recipe, it's very important to use a pot with a tight-fitting lid, to minimize the escape of steam. This soup starts out with very little water, and during most of its cooking it will seem like a very thick stew. However, additional water will be released by the vegetables as they cook, and the soup will thin out quite a bit at the end when the dairy ingredients are added.

Nondairy Corn Chowder

Follow Corn Chowder recipe, but substitute 3 tablespoons safflower oil for the 4 tablespoons butter. Omit sour cream, cream cheese, and milk. Use instead $1\frac{1}{2}$ cups raw cashew pieces and 1 cup water.

In blender, blend cashews and water until very smooth. Add to soup at last step, with nutritional yeast and chives.

This nondairy formula may be used in other creamy dairy soups as well. It goes especially well with corn chowder, because corn and cashews both have a sweet flavor. Experiment with other soups, too, but don't expect the flavor to be exactly the same as when using dairy.

When substituting oil for butter, use $\frac{1}{2}$–$\frac{3}{4}$ the amount of butter called for. If a recipe calls for 4 tablespoons butter, use only 2–3 tablespoons oil.

Cream of Carrot

Spencer Windbiel

Cooking time: 1 hr. Makes 4 qts.

This soup has the pleasant sweet taste of fresh carrots, as well as a carroty color.

8 c. water
4 Tbsp. butter
1 bay leaf
2 c. chopped yellow onion
$5\frac{1}{2}$ c. carrots—2 c. quartered lengthwise, then diced into $\frac{1}{4}''$ thick pieces; $3\frac{1}{2}$ c. sliced into $\frac{1}{4}''$ rounds
$\frac{1}{3}$ c. chopped green pepper
2 c. chopped celery
2 med. cloves garlic, pressed
2 c. fresh carrot juice, or 2 c. chopped raw carrot blended with 1 c. water in an electric blender until pureed

2 c. russet potato (unpeeled), chopped into fairly large chunks
1 Tbsp. crumbled basil
2 tsp. Spike
1 tsp. granulated garlic (optional, or to taste)
$\frac{3}{4}$ c. sour cream
$\frac{1}{4}$ c. (2 oz.) cream cheese
$\frac{1}{4}$ c. milk
1 10-oz. pkg. frozen peas, rinsed under hot water to thaw, or 2 c. shelled fresh peas, lightly steamed until tender and bright green
2 Tbsp. dried chives
sea salt to taste

In a 5- or 6-quart pot, bring to a boil: water, butter, bay leaf, onion, diced carrots, green pepper, celery, and pressed garlic. Reduce heat to simmer, and cook, covered, about 20 minutes, or until carrots are quite tender.

To this stock add the sliced carrot rounds. Bring soup to a boil again, lower heat and continue simmering, covered, until carrot rounds are just tender, about 15 minutes.

Add carrot juice or carrot puree, potatoes, basil, Spike, and granulated garlic. Bring to a boil, then reduce heat to simmer and cook only until potatoes can be pierced easily with a fork, about 10 minutes. Remove from heat.

In blender, blend together sour cream, cream cheese, and milk until smooth. Add to soup along with peas, chives, and salt. Return soup to stove and heat gently, at lowest heat (stirring often), just until hot. Serve.

Cream of Green Things

Paul Lewin

Cooking time: 1¼ hrs.   Makes 3–3½ qts.

Green vegetables are the obvious inspiration for this refreshing soup. The cabbage, summer squash, spinach, and watercress are essential for the base—beyond that, you may substitute your favorite green vegetables with good result.

6½ c. water
1 lg. bay leaf
½ c. dried green split peas
1½ c. (1 lg.) diced summer squash
    (the round, pale green type)
¾ c. diced green cabbage
1 Tbsp. minced fresh cilantro
    (optional)
⅓ lb. broccoli—diced stems; bite-sized flowerettes
1 c. finely chopped fresh spinach
    (wash well)
½ c. finely chopped watercress
1 c. diced celery
1 c. diced green onions
2 tsp. cut thyme leaf (not powdered)

1 c. fresh green beans, chopped
    into 2" lengths
1 c. zucchini, sliced into
    ½" rounds
¼ c. minced fresh parsley
1 10-oz. pkg. frozen peas, rinsed
    under hot water to thaw, or
    2 c. shelled fresh peas, lightly
    steamed until tender and
    bright green
1 Tbsp. dried chives
3 Tbsp. butter
1 c. half and half
sea salt to taste

Prepare broccoli by first discarding woody part of stem. Cut flower tops at 2" length, and reserve for later. Dice remaining stems and leaves.

In a 5- or 6-quart pot, bring to a boil: water, bay leaf, split peas, summer squash, cabbage, cilantro, diced broccoli stems, spinach, watercress, celery, green onions, and thyme. Reduce heat and simmer, tightly covered, for 30–40 minutes, or until split peas are quite tender and vegetables very soft.

Remove from heat. Let cool slightly, then pour into heat-proof blender container. Cover with a tight-fitting lid (careful—it's hot!), and blend until smooth, just a few seconds. You may have to do this in two batches.

Pour blended stock back into soup pot. Add green beans, zucchini, broccoli flowerettes, and parsley. Bring heat to simmer, and cook, covered, 10–15 minutes, or until vegetables are slightly tender. Add peas and chives, and simmer another 5 minutes.

Reduce to lowest heat. Add butter, half and half, and sea salt. Serve.

Cream of Tomato Soupreme

Kristine Molasky-McCallister

Cooking time: 45 min.   Makes 3 qts.

An elegant dinner-party soup, rich and tomatoey.

5 c. tomato puree—$2\frac{1}{2}$ lbs. (6 lg.) chopped, unpeeled ripe tomatoes (or 2 1-lb. cans stewed tomatoes and 1 c. water), blended until smooth
1 c. thinly sliced celery
$\frac{1}{4}$ c. dry red wine
2 sm. cloves garlic, pressed or minced
1 16-oz. can diced tomatoes, or stewed whole tomatoes, chopped (include juice)
2 c. water

12 oz. tomato paste
$2\frac{1}{2}$ tsp. crumbled basil
$2\frac{1}{2}$ tsp. olive oil
1 c. (1 med.) diced yellow onion
$\frac{1}{2}$ c. (1 sm.) diced green pepper
1 bay leaf
1 c. ($\frac{1}{2}$ pt.) sour cream
2 Tbsp. butter
16 oz. half and half
1 tsp. sea salt, or to taste
pinch of cayenne, or dash of black pepper, to taste

In a 4- or 5-quart pot, bring to a boil: tomato puree, celery, and wine. Simmer, tightly covered, about 20 minutes, or until puree is deep red and celery slightly tender.

Add garlic, diced tomatoes, water, tomato paste, and basil. Continue simmering about 15–20 minutes, or until celery is very tender.

Meanwhile, gently heat olive oil in a heavy skillet. Sauté the onion, green pepper, and bay leaf for about 10–15 minutes, stirring frequently, until onions are golden and both vegetables are quite tender.

Add onion mixture to soup. Turn burner to lowest heat. Add sour cream, butter, and half and half. Add salt and pepper, and adjust seasonings to taste. Serve, garnished with small crackers if desired.

Cream of Zucchini

Micki Besancon
Bob Goldberg

Easy
Cooking time: 1¼ hrs.   Makes 5 qts.

Cooking zucchini into the base of this soup for a relatively long time contributes to its rich flavor.

8 c. water
6 c. (3 lg.) diced russet potato
  (unpeeled)
8 c. (5 lg.) zucchini—5 c. diced;
  3 c. sliced in thin rounds
2 c. (2 lg.) diced yellow onion
2 Tbsp. butter
2 Tbsp. Jensen's broth powder
½ tsp. whole celery seed

¼ c. minced fresh parsley
1½ tsp. granulated garlic
1½ tsp. crumbled basil leaf
1 c. sour cream
1 c. milk
3 oz. cream cheese
¼ lb. grated sharp Cheddar
2 tsp. Spike, or to taste
dash cayenne pepper

In a 6- to 8-quart pot, bring to a boil: water, potatoes, diced zucchini, onion, butter, Jensen's broth powder, and celery seed. Reduce heat to medium and cook, tightly covered, 45 minutes, or until vegetables begin to dissolve.

Add parsley, zucchini rounds, garlic, and basil, and simmer 10–15 minutes, or until zucchini rounds are just tender. Turn burner to lowest heat.

Blend sour cream, milk, cream cheese, and Cheddar cheese in blender until smooth. Add to soup, and heat gently, until very hot but not boiling. Add Spike and cayenne pepper to taste. Serve.

Creamy Broccoli Rice (Wedding Soup)

Paul Lewin

Cooking time: 1½ hrs.   Makes 3½ qts.

Also known as "Wedding Soup," it was named for a wedding we catered, where it was quite popular.

8 c. water
⅓ c. dried green split peas
½ c. finely shredded green cabbage
½ c. finely shredded pale green summer squash (may substitute zucchini or yellow squash)
2 bay leaves
1 tsp. ground rosemary
½ c. finely chopped fresh spinach leaves
½ c. diced yellow onion
¾ c. diced celery
¾ c. sliced fresh mushrooms
¾ c. long grain brown rice, uncooked

2 med. cloves garlic, pressed or minced
1½ lbs. broccoli—2 c. diced stems; 4 c. bite-sized flowerettes
1 lb. cauliflower—1 c. diced core; 2 c. bite-sized flowerettes
1 tsp. crumbled basil leaf
4 Tbsp. butter
3 Tbsp. cream
¼ c. milk
1½ tsp. Vege-Sal, or to taste
1 tsp. sea salt, or to taste
1 tsp. onion powder, or to taste

In a 5- or 6-quart pot, bring to a boil: water, split peas, cabbage, squash, bay leaves, ½ teaspoon of the rosemary, spinach, onion, celery, and mushrooms. Reduce heat and simmer, covered, until vegetables are quite tender and peas very soft, about 40 minutes.

Prepare broccoli and cauliflower by discarding woody stems, finely dicing remaining stems (or core), and breaking flowerettes into bite-sized pieces. Set flowerettes aside for later.

Add rice, garlic, broccoli and cauliflower stems. Continue simmering on low heat, covered, about 25 minutes, or until rice is a little tender. Add broccoli and cauliflower flowerettes and basil and continue simmering 15–20 minutes, or until rice is tender (flowerettes should be just tender, not overcooked).

Turn off heat. Add butter, cream, milk, Vege-Sal, sea salt, onion powder, and remaining $\frac{1}{2}$ teaspoon rosemary. Adjust seasonings to taste. Serve.

Creamy Curried Split Pea

Janice Cook Migliaccio

Cooking time: 1 hr.   Makes 5 qts.

Thick, rich, and luscious, with the flavor of curry and other Indian spices. It is spicy tasting, but not too hot.

$3\frac{1}{4}$ c. ($1\frac{1}{2}$ lbs.) dried green split peas	1 tsp. ground cumin
10 c. water	$\frac{1}{2}$ tsp. ground coriander
1 c. diced yam (unpeeled)	$\frac{1}{2}$ tsp. turmeric
$2\frac{1}{2}$ c. chopped yellow onion	$\frac{1}{4}$ tsp. cinnamon
3 c. celery, sliced $\frac{1}{4}''$ thick (include leaves)	$\frac{1}{4}$ tsp. cardamom
2 whole bay leaves	$\frac{1}{8}$ tsp. nutmeg
1 tsp. cut thyme leaf	1 10-oz. pkg. frozen peas, rinsed
2 Tbsp. curry powder	under hot water to thaw, or
1 c. carrot, sliced in $\frac{1}{4}''$ rounds	$2\frac{1}{4}$ c. shelled fresh peas, lightly
$\frac{1}{4}$ c. ($\frac{1}{2}$ cube) butter	steamed until tender and
2 Tbsp. tamari	bright green
1 Tbsp. Spike	1 c. sour cream
1 Tbsp. dried parsley	6 oz. sharp Cheddar cheese,
1 Tbsp. granulated garlic	shredded ($1\frac{1}{2}$ c. packed)
	3 Tbsp. curry powder, or to taste

In a 6-quart pot, bring to a boil: split peas, water, yam, onion, celery, bay leaves, thyme, and the 2 tablespoons curry powder.

Lower heat and simmer, covered, stirring occasionally, until split peas begin to break down, about $\frac{1}{2}$ hour.

Add carrots, butter, tamari, Spike, parsley, garlic, cumin, coriander, turmeric, cinnamon, cardamom, and nutmeg. Simmer, covered, stirring occasionally, until carrots are just tender. Turn heat to lowest flame.

Blend sour cream, Cheddar cheese, and a little of the hot soup broth in blender until smooth. Careful! It's hot. Add cheese mixture and fresh or frozen peas back to soup in pot. Heat gently—do not boil. Stir often.

Add more curry powder, to taste. Add water (1–2 cups) if necessary; soup should be fairly thick and creamy. Serve.

Note: Use a pot with a tight-fitting lid—split peas absorb lots of water, so you don't want to lose too much to evaporation. This is why water may need to be added later. Also, curry powders vary tremendously from brand to brand. Two tablespoons go in at the beginning to really get the flavor in, but later add more (about 3 tablespoons, depending on taste) carefully. I used a fairly mild curry powder.

Creamy Potato Leek

Marsha Stamp

Easy
Cooking time: 45 min.   Makes 4 qts.

Leeks have a delicate, mild onion flavor that enjoys the company of potatoes.

8 c. water
12 c. (6 med.) russet potatoes (unpeeled)—8 c. finely diced; 4 c. chopped into $\frac{3}{4}$" cubes
3 c. (3 med.) thinly sliced leeks (wash well—see "Washing, Soaking, and Cleaning" section; use both green and white parts)
3–3$\frac{1}{2}$ c. (5 lg. stalks) chopped celery

4 Tbsp. butter
3–4 lg. cloves garlic, pressed or minced
2 tsp. dill weed
1 Tbsp. crumbled basil
$\frac{1}{2}$ tsp. ground celery seed
1 c. sour cream
1 Tbsp. Spike, or to taste
Vege-Sal or sea salt to taste

In a 5- or 6-quart pot, bring to a boil: water, diced potatoes, leeks, and celery. Simmer, covered, until potatoes are very tender and begin to dissolve, about 30 minutes. Stir occasionally.

Add butter, cubed potatoes, garlic, dill, basil, and celery seed. Simmer, covered, until potato cubes are just tender. Turn burner to lowest heat.

In blender, blend the sour cream with just enough soup broth to make a smooth paste. Stir into soup. Season with Spike and sea salt, to taste, and adjust other seasonings if desired. Heat gently just until very hot, but not boiling. Serve.

Creamy Spinach Mushroom

Paul Lewin

Cooking time: 45 min.   Makes 4 qts.

A pretty soup: buttery broth attractively filled with sliced mushrooms and bits of spinach.

8 c. water
½ lb. (3 c.) sliced mushrooms—
  reserve 1 c.
2 c. (1 lg.) yellow onion, sliced in
  thin half-circles
1½ c. (2 lg. stalks) thinly sliced
  celery
2 lbs. finely chopped fresh
  spinach (wash well—see
  "Washing, Soaking, and
  Cleaning" section)—reserve ½
1 c. diced green onions—reserve
  ¼ c. for garnish
4 Tbsp. butter

2 Tbsp. tamari
1 Tbsp. crumbled basil leaf
1 Tbsp. crumbled oregano leaf
½ tsp. ground celery seed
¼ tsp. black pepper, or dash of
  cayenne
4 oz. grated sharp Cheddar
3 oz. cream cheese
1 c. sour cream
2 tsp. Spike
2 tsp. Dr. Bronner's seasoning
  powder
sea salt (or tamari) to taste

In a 5- or 6-quart pot, bring to a boil: water, 2 cups of the mushrooms, onions, celery, and ½ of the spinach. Reduce heat and simmer, covered, about 20 minutes, or until onions and celery are tender.

Add reserved mushrooms and spinach, ¾ cup of the green onions, butter, tamari, basil, oregano, celery seed, and pepper. Simmer about 10 minutes.

Turn burner to lowest heat. In blender container, place Cheddar cheese, cream cheese, and sour cream, and enough of the hot soup broth that the mixture will blend, about ¾ cup. (Make sure blender lid is on tight!) Blend until smooth, then add mixture back to soup and heat gently for a few minutes. Add Spike and Dr. Bronner's powder. Season to taste with tamari and sea salt, if desired. Serve sprinkled with green onions.

Creamy Sweet Potato

Janice Cook Migliaccio

Cooking time: $1\frac{1}{4}$ hrs.   Makes 4 qts.

This soup receives its natural sweet flavor from yams, sweet potatoes, carrots, basil, and tarragon.

8 c. water
2 tsp. cut thyme leaf
2 bay leaves
3 c. diced yellow onion
$2\frac{1}{2}$ lbs. yams and/or sweet potatoes ($1\frac{1}{4}$ lbs. of each if possible)—6 c. diced; 2 c. cut in $\frac{1}{4}$″ thick half-circles
2 c. thinly sliced celery
2 c. (1 med.) chopped russet potato
1 c. carrots, sliced in $\frac{1}{4}$″ rounds
2 tsp. basil

1 tsp. tarragon
1 10-oz. pkg. frozen peas, rinsed under hot water to thaw, or $2\frac{1}{4}$ c. shelled fresh peas, lightly steamed until tender and bright green
2 Tbsp. minced fresh parsley
1 c. sour cream
$\frac{1}{2}$ c. milk
2 tsp. Spike
2 tsp. sea salt, to taste
2 Tbsp. dried chives

Bring to a boil: water, thyme, bay leaves, onions, diced yams and/or sweet potatoes. Lower heat to medium and cook, covered, about 30 minutes, until sweet potatoes begin to break down and form a broth. Stir occasionally.

Add celery and russet potato, and continue cooking 10 minutes.

Add sweet potato and yam half-circles, carrots, basil, and tarragon. Lower heat and simmer, covered, until carrots and sweet potato pieces are tender, about 10–15 minutes. Stir occasionally.

Add peas and parsley, and simmer 5 minutes.

Turn burner to lowest heat. Blend sour cream and milk together in blender container, and add to soup along with Spike, salt, and chives. Heat gently, stirring often, until soup is hot but not boiling. Adjust seasonings to taste. Serve.

Creamy Winter Grains

Erly Lawrence

Cooking time: 1 hr.   Makes 3½ qts.

One bowl of this makes a hearty winter meal.

⅓ c. whole wheat berries, presoaked
8 c. water
½ c. lentils
¼ c. hulled barley
¼ c. short grain brown rice
3 Tbsp. butter
1½ tsp. thyme
1 c. cubed red or russet potato
1 c. carrots, sliced in ¼" rounds
1 c. sliced celery
1 c. diced yellow onion
½ tsp. ground celery seed
1 lg. clove garlic, pressed
2 tsp. Jensen's broth powder
1 tsp. granulated onion
1 tsp. granulated garlic
2 Tbsp. dried parsley

3 Tbsp. tamari
⅔ c. corn, fresh or frozen (if frozen, rinse under hot water to thaw; if fresh, lightly steam until tender and color bright)
⅔ c. peas, fresh or frozen (if frozen, rinse under hot water to thaw; if fresh, lightly steam until tender and color bright)
1 c. additional water
2 oz. (¼ c.) cream cheese
⅔ c. sour cream
¼ lb. sharp Cheddar, grated (⅔ c., packed)
⅛ tsp. cayenne, or to taste
1 tsp. Vege-Sal, or to taste
fresh parsley sprigs, for garnish

Soak wheat berries in 2 cups water for 6 hours or overnight. Drain wheat in a strainer, reserving the soaking water; add fresh water to it to equal 8 cups. In a 4- or 5-quart pot, bring water, wheat berries, lentils, barley, rice, butter, and thyme to a boil. Reduce heat, cover, and simmer 20 minutes.

Add potato, carrots, celery, onion, celery seed, and fresh garlic. Bring again to a simmer, and continue to cook, covered, until vegetables and grains are tender, about 30 minutes, stirring occasionally.

Add Jensen's broth powder, granulated onion, granulated garlic, dried parsley, tamari, corn, and peas. (Soup will be quite thick.) Reduce to lowest heat.

In blender, blend 1 cup water, cream cheese, sour cream, and Cheddar cheese until smooth. Add to soup. Heat gently, stirring, just until very hot; do not boil.

Add cayenne and Vege-Sal, to taste. Serve garnished with sprigs of fresh parsley.

Curried Millet Vegetable

Sondra McCaffrey

Cooking time: 50–60 min.   Makes $3\frac{1}{2}$–4 qts.

For curry lovers, this soup has a wonderful exotic flavor and rich color.

8 c. water
$2\frac{1}{4}$ c. (2 or 3 med.) chopped
   yellow onion
$1\frac{1}{2}$ c. chopped celery
1 c. carrot, sliced in $\frac{1}{4}''$ rounds
2 Tbsp. olive oil
2 med. cloves garlic, pressed or
   minced
1 c. hulled millet, uncooked

$\frac{3}{4}$ lb. broccoli—$1\frac{1}{2}$ c. sliced stems;
   2 c. bite-sized flowerettes
2 Tbsp. curry powder
1 tsp. crumbled basil leaf
$\frac{1}{2}$ tsp. cut thyme leaf
5 Tbsp. tamari
2 tsp. Spike
$\frac{1}{4}$ tsp. garlic powder

In a 5- or 6-quart pot, bring to a boil: water, onion, celery, carrot, olive oil, and fresh garlic. Reduce heat and simmer, covered, about 15 minutes, or until onion is slightly tender.

To prepare broccoli, discard woody stem ends, cut bite-sized flowerettes attractively and set aside, and slice remaining stem.

Add millet, broccoli stems, curry, basil, and thyme. Bring to second boil, then reduce heat and simmer, covered, until millet is tender, about 20–25 minutes.

Add broccoli flowerettes, tamari, Spike, and garlic powder. If needed, up to $2\frac{1}{2}$ cups more water may be added—soup should be medium thick. Simmer until broccoli tops are just tender and bright green, about 10 minutes. Adjust seasonings; add additional curry powder if desired. Serve.

Dear Aunt Lilly's Lima Bean

Spencer Windbiel

Easy
Cooking time: 1 hr., 20 min.   Makes 4–4½ qts.

A meatless version of the original, this recipe is inspired by Spencer's dear Aunt Lilly.

10 c. water
3⅓ c. (1¼ lbs.) dried lg. lima beans, presoaked
1 lg. bay leaf
1½ c. chopped yellow onion
1 c. carrots, sliced in ¼" rounds
1½ c. chopped celery (include finely diced leaves)
2 c. (1 lg.) chopped russet potato (unpeeled)

4 Tbsp. butter or margarine
2 Tbsp. Spike
1½ tsp. basil
2 tsp. granulated garlic
1¼ tsp. bakon bits, or 1 tsp. bakon flavored yeast powder
¼ c. thinly sliced green onion
2 Tbsp. minced fresh parsley
½ tsp. salt, or to taste
black pepper or cayenne to taste

Soak lima beans for 6 hours or overnight in 10 cups water. Drain and discard soaking water. Place beans in 5- or 6-quart pot with 10 cups fresh water, bay leaf, and yellow onion. Bring to a boil, cover. Simmer, stirring occasionally, until beans are slightly tender, about 40 minutes.

Add carrots and celery, and continue to simmer, covered, for 15 minutes, or until carrots and beans are quite tender, but still intact.

Add potato, butter, Spike, basil, and garlic. Simmer about 10–15 minutes, stirring occasionally, until potatoes pierce easily with a fork.

Turn burner to lowest heat. Ladle out 1½ cups of the hot soup broth, avoiding beans and vegetables if possible. In a blender, blend broth with bakon bits or bakon yeast until smooth. Add this mixture back to the soup, along with the green onions, parsley, salt, and just enough pepper to add a little spunk to the soup. Simmer gently 5 minutes, serve.

Eggplant Parmesan Soup

Micki Besancon
Sharon Carson

Cooking time: 1 hr.   Makes 5 qts.

Serve with garlic bread and a dark green or antipasto salad for a superb Italian meal.

6 c. water
3 c. (l lg.) diced russet potato (unpeeled)
2 c. chopped yellow onion
1 lg. bay leaf
$\frac{1}{2}$ c. ea. red and green pepper, or 1 c. of either if one is not available
1$\frac{1}{2}$ c. chopped celery
3$\frac{1}{2}$–4 c. (1 lb.) cubed, peeled eggplant
$\frac{3}{4}$ lb. cauliflower—1 c. finely diced stem; 2 c. bite-sized flowerettes
1$\frac{1}{4}$ c. sliced zucchini

1$\frac{1}{4}$ c. sliced yellow squash (substitute zucchini if yellow squash unavailable)
1 15-oz. can tomato sauce
1 12-oz. can tomato paste
2 Tbsp. sesame seeds
2 tsp. bakon bits
2 tsp. crumbled basil leaf
$\frac{1}{2}$ tsp. granulated garlic
$\frac{3}{4}$ c. uncooked whole grain elbow macaroni
$\frac{1}{4}$ c. grated Parmesan cheese
cayenne to taste
$\frac{1}{2}$ tsp. sea salt, or to taste

In a 6- or 8-quart pot, bring to a boil: water, potato, onion, and bay leaf. Reduce heat to medium and cook tightly covered about 20 minutes, or until potato is very soft and begins to dissolve.

Add green and red pepper, celery, eggplant, and cauliflower stems. Bring to second boil; reduce heat and simmer, covered, about 15 minutes, or until eggplant is tender but firm.

Add zucchini, yellow squash, cauliflowerettes, tomato sauce, tomato paste, sesame seeds, bakon bits, basil, and garlic. Simmer, covered, 10–15 minutes, or until squash is tender.

Meanwhile, cook elbow macaroni in water according to package directions until al dente, or just tender. Rinse and drain.

Turn burner to lowest heat. Add cooked macaroni, Parmesan cheese, cayenne, and sea salt. Adjust seasonings to taste. Serve.

Enchilada Soup

Bob Goldberg

Easy, if using prepared ingredients
Cooking time: long version, $1\frac{1}{4}$ hrs.
               short version, $\frac{1}{2}$ hr.   Makes 4–$4\frac{1}{2}$ qts.

There are two different ways to make this soup, both resulting in the same basic flavor. The long way uses fresh beans and homemade enchilada sauce; the short way uses canned beans and canned enchilada sauce. Both are rich and flavorful.

$\frac{2}{3}$ c. ($\frac{1}{4}$ lb.) dried pinto beans, presoaked

$\frac{1}{4}$ c. ($\frac{1}{8}$ lb.) dried kidney beans, presoaked

(to save time, you may substitute 1 19-oz. can of Las Palmas chili beans for the pinto and kidney bean combination above)

3–4 c. water

1 tsp. sea salt

2 c. diced yellow onion

4 $2\frac{1}{4}$-oz. cans sliced black olives (2 c., packed)

3 15-oz. cans tomato sauce (Spanish-style or regular)

$1\frac{3}{4}$ c. homemade enchilada sauce (recipe follows), or 1 19-oz. can Las Palmas Enchilada Sauce

1 tsp. granulated garlic

2 c. (2 med.) chopped fresh tomato

2 c. sour cream

$\frac{1}{2}$ lb. grated Cheddar cheese

$\frac{1}{4}$ lb. grated jack cheese

3 Tbsp. dried chives

$\frac{1}{3}$ c. sliced green onion

$\frac{1}{2}$ doz. corn tortillas, cut in wedges

2 oz. natural barbecue-flavor corn chips (optional)

(If using canned beans, disregard the first paragraph.)
Soak pinto and kidney beans in 4 cups water for 6 hours or overnight. Drain and discard soaking water. In a 3- or 4-quart pot, bring beans to a boil with 3 cups water and sea salt. Reduce heat and simmer, covered, until beans are quite tender, about 40–45 minutes. Add more water during cooking if necessary. (Kidney beans may take a little longer than the pintos to cook.) Drain beans and set aside.

In a 5- or 6-quart pot, bring to a simmer: diced onion, sliced olives, tomato sauce, and enchilada sauce. Simmer, covered, stirring occasionally, just until mixture is very hot and onions are slightly tender (about 10–15 minutes).

Add beans (fresh or canned), garlic (omit if using canned enchilada sauce), chopped tomatoes, and sour cream. Continue heating, at very low heat, stirring frequently to keep beans from settling. (Settling may cause them to burn easily.) When mixture is again very hot (but *not* boiling), stir in grated cheese. Continue stirring until cheese is thoroughly melted. Turn off heat.

Add chives, green onions, and corn tortillas. Add corn chips if desired (they'll make the soup thicker and even more flavorful, but you may like it as is). Serve.

Enchilada Sauce

$2\frac{1}{2}$ c. water
1 oz. (2 lg.) dried red New Mex-
    ico or California chili pods
1 8-oz. can tomato sauce (Span-
    ish-style or regular)
$\frac{1}{2}$ tsp. chili powder
$\frac{1}{8}$ tsp. granulated garlic
$\frac{1}{8}$ tsp. cayenne
$\frac{1}{8}$ tsp. cumin
$\frac{1}{8}$ tsp. sea salt

Break stems off chili pods and wash if necessary. In a small pot, cover chilies with 1 cup water. Bring to a boil, and simmer, covered, until chilies are soft, about 15–20 minutes. (To test for doneness, poke chili with a dull knife. If it pierces easily and starts to separate, it's done.)

In a tightly covered blender container, (careful, this mixture is hot) blend water and cooked chilies *thoroughly*. Skins should be totally blended; blend at high speed for at least 30 seconds. Pour mixture through a coarse sieve to remove seeds and any unblended pulp. (Press pulp firmly with the back of a spoon to force out all the juice.)

Return blended chili mixture to small pot. Add tomato sauce, chili powder, garlic, cayenne, cumin, and salt, and simmer gently, covered, until flavors are well blended, about 5 minutes. Makes 2–2$\frac{1}{2}$ cups. Use in Enchilada Soup, or with enchiladas.

French Onion

Brion Levitsky
Sondra McCaffrey
Janice Cook Migliaccio

Cooking time: 45 min.–1 hr.   Makes 2 qts.

A simple, classic soup for onion lovers.

8 c. yellow onion, cut in thin half-circles
4 Tbsp. ($\frac{1}{2}$ cube) butter
6 c. water
2 lg. cloves garlic, pressed or minced
$\frac{1}{4}$ c. tamari

2 Tbsp. Dr. Bronner's seasoning powder
garlic croutons (recipe follows)
$\frac{1}{4}$ lb. shredded Gruyere, Swiss, mozzarella, or Cheddar cheese, or several Tbsps. Parmesan cheese

In a large skillet, melt 2 tablespoons of butter. Add and sauté 4 cups of the onions, until they're a deep brown, but *not* burned. The trick is to cook them till they're well-browned and tender, yet still have a little firmness. (If the onions do burn, start over—burned onions will ruin the flavor.) Repeat this step with the remaining butter and onions.

In a 3- or 4-quart pot, place all the sautéed onions, the garlic, and the 6 cups water. Bring to a boil; reduce heat and simmer, covered, about 20 minutes, or until soup broth is quite flavorful. Turn burner to lowest heat.

Add tamari and Bronner's seasoning powder. Add a little more water if desired.

Serve hot as is or topped with garlic croutons and shredded cheese. (If soup is hot the cheese will melt right in.) Or pour the soup into oven-proof serving bowls, top with croutons and cheese, and place under the broiler until cheese is melted and bubbly.

Garlic Croutons

4 Tbsp. lightly salted butter,
　softened
2 tsp. garlic powder
4 slices whole grain bread
dried parsley

Preheat oven to 350°. Mix softened butter with garlic powder. Spread generously on bread, and sprinkle lightly with dried parsley flakes. Cut into $\frac{3}{4}''$ cubes. Place on a baking sheet and bake until dry and crisp, about 20 minutes. Allow to cool uncovered in a dry place before storing in a closed container, or use immediately.

Makes enough croutons for 4 large bowls or 8 cups of soup.

Garbanzo Party (or Kidney Bean Fling)

Hedy Kelho

Easy
Cooking time: 1 hr., 20 min.   Makes 4½–5 qts.

A brightly colored vegetable soup with the addition of garbanzo or kidney beans.

2 c. dried garbanzo beans (chickpeas), presoaked
8 c. water
2 c. chopped yellow onion
1½ c. chopped celery
3 med. cloves garlic, pressed or minced
2 tsp. sea salt
1 c. thinly sliced carrots (⅛″ thick), cut on diagonal
2 tsp. crumbled basil leaf

1 tsp. crumbled oregano leaf
1½ c. shredded red cabbage
1 c. grated zucchini
1 c. grated yellow squash (substitute zucchini if yellow squash unavailable)
1 1-lb. can stewed tomatoes (drain and chop tomatoes coarsely)
3 Tbsp. tamari, or to taste

Check beans carefully, discarding rocks if any, and wash thoroughly. Soak beans in 4 cups water for 12 hours.

In a 6- or 8-quart pot, bring to a boil: 8 cups water, presoaked beans, onion, celery, and garlic. Reduce heat to medium-low and simmer, tightly covered, about 25 minutes. Add sea salt and continue simmering, covered, until beans are tender, about 25–30 minutes.

Add carrots, basil, and oregano. Simmer 10 minutes.

Add red cabbage, zucchini, yellow squash, tomatoes and additional water, as needed, and simmer until added veggies are tender, about 5–10 minutes. Add tamari. Adjust seasonings to taste. Serve.

Variation: Kidney Bean Fling

Substitute kidney beans for the garbanzo beans. Keep the rest of the recipe the same; you may want to add an additional 2 tablespoons tamari.

Gazpacho

Janice Cook Migliaccio

Easy
Preparation time: $\frac{1}{2}$ hr.   Makes 3 qts.

Serve this soup chilled—it's wonderfully refreshing in warm weather. As much a salad as it is a soup.

$1\frac{3}{4}$ c. (2 sm.) diced yellow onion— reserve $\frac{1}{2}$ c.
$3\frac{1}{2}$ c. (2 lg.) peeled cucumber, cut into $\frac{1}{2}''$ cubes—reserve $1\frac{1}{2}$ c.
$1\frac{1}{4}$ c. (2 sm.) diced green pepper—reserve $\frac{1}{4}$ c.
4 c. (3 or 4 lg.) diced fresh tomato (unpeeled)—reserve 2 c.
3 Tbsp. unrefined olive oil
2 Tbsp. fresh lemon juice, or to taste

2 med. cloves garlic, pressed or minced
1 Tbsp. honey, or to taste
pinch of cayenne pepper, to taste
1 tsp. dill weed
3 Tbsp. eggless mayonnaise
4 c. tomato juice
2–4 Tbsp. each of minced parsley, and chopped cilantro or watercress, as garnish

Blend all but reserved ingredients and garnish in blender briefly, until just barely smooth. (Do this in 2 or 3 batches.) Stir in reserved $\frac{1}{2}$ cup onion, $1\frac{1}{2}$ c. cucumber, $\frac{1}{4}$ c. green pepper, and 2 c. tomato, or leave in separate bowls and let people add them if they desire. Chill thoroughly before serving. Garnish with parsley and cilantro or watercress.

Grandma's Celery Potato

Grandma Clara Krug
Carol Krug Cook
Janice Cook Migliaccio

Easy
Cooking time: 1 hr.   Makes $3\frac{1}{2}$ qts.

This soup goes back at least four generations. I know it best from eating at my grandmother's house, though it was made by her mother and my mother too. I recreated it at Follow Your Heart, and figured out a written recipe for you to try too. It's very simple to prepare—the secret is not to overcook it, so the potatoes remain a little firm.

3 Tbsp. salted butter
$2\frac{1}{4}$ c. (2 med.) yellow onions, quartered, then thinly sliced
4 c. (5–6 lg. stalks) celery, cut in half lengthwise, then thinly sliced (include finely chopped leaves)
1 lg. bay leaf
6 c. water

6 c. (3 med.) russet potatoes (un-peeled), quartered lengthwise, then sliced $\frac{1}{4}''$ thick
$2\frac{1}{4}$ c. milk
$1\frac{1}{2}$ tsp. sea salt or celery salt, or to taste
dash of black pepper, or a pinch of cayenne, to taste
fresh parsley sprigs, as garnish

In a heavy-bottomed 5- or 6-quart pot, melt butter over low heat. Add onions and celery, and sauté gently, stirring frequently, about 10 minutes. (Vegetables should be golden and slightly tender, but not brown.)

Add bay leaf and 2 cups of the water. Cover and simmer on low heat, about 30 minutes, or until onions and celery are very tender.

Add potatoes and remaining 4 cups water. Bring to a boil, then reduce heat and simmer for 10–15 minutes, or until potatoes are quite tender but still intact. Turn burner to lowest heat.

Add milk, along with salt and pepper to taste. Heat, stirring gently, just until hot but not boiling. Serve garnished with sprigs of fresh parsley.

Irish Stew

Kathleen Maloney

Easy
Cooking time: 1 hr.   Makes 4 qts.

At Follow Your Heart, we usually serve this soup with the added cream, but you can omit it and use margarine instead of butter for a nondairy soup.

8 c. water
2 c. (2–3 lg. stalks) chopped celery
3 c. (2 med.) diced yellow onion
6½ c. (3 med.) russet potatoes (unpeeled)—4 c. diced; 2½ c. cut in ¾" cubes
3 c. (1 sm. head) green cabbage—1 c. diced; 2 c. thinly sliced
2 lg. bay leaves
1 tsp. thyme leaf, cut (*not* ground or whole)

1 tsp. crumbled basil leaf
½ tsp. ground celery seed
2 c. (2 med.) carrots, quartered lengthwise, then sliced ¼" thick
½ c. minced fresh parsley
2 tsp. sea salt
4 Tbsp. butter or margarine
dash of black pepper, or a pinch of cayenne, to taste
2–4 Tbsp. cream (optional)

In a 5- or 6-quart pot, bring to a boil: water, celery, onion, diced potatoes, diced cabbage, bay leaves, and thyme. Turn heat to medium. Cover and cook ½ hour, or until vegetables are tender.

Add basil, celery seed, and carrots. Lower heat and continue simmering about 15 minutes, or until carrots are just tender, and other vegetables have begun dissolving into broth.

Add cubed potatoes, sliced cabbage, parsley, salt, and butter or margarine. Simmer, covered, stirring occasionally, until potato cubes are just tender, about 10–15 minutes. Turn burner to lowest heat.

Add pepper, and cream if desired. Adjust seasonings to taste. (If you add cream it may cool the soup a bit, so heat gently, stirring, just until hot, without boiling.) Serve.

Italian Vegetable

Janice Cook Migliaccio

Cooking time: 1 hr.   Makes 5 qts.

A hearty Italian soup, best prepared in summer when fresh tomatoes, eggplant, and squash are plentiful.

¼ c. unrefined olive oil
3 c. yellow onion, cut in thin half-circles
½ c. chopped green pepper
4 c. eggplant, peeled and cut into bite-sized chunks
8 c. tomato puree—4 lbs. chopped, unpeeled ripe tomatoes (or 3 1-lb. cans whole or diced tomatoes and 2 c. water) blended until smooth
4 c. water
1 c. carrot, sliced diagonally or in rounds, ¼″ thick
2 c. thinly sliced celery
½ c. finely chopped fresh parsley
8 med. cloves garlic, pressed or minced
1 Tbsp. finely crumbled oregano leaf

2 tsp. finely crumbled basil leaf
¼ tsp. ground rosemary
1½ tsp. granulated garlic, or to taste
1 tsp. apple cider vinegar
5 c. mixed summer squash, zucchini, yellow squash, cut into rounds or chunks
3 Tbsp. tamari
1–2 tsp. sea salt, to taste
1 Tbsp. honey, or to taste (depends on flavor of tomatoes—canned puree is often sweeter than fresh)
grated Parmesan or mozzarella (optional)
1 c. cooked garbanzo beans (optional)
garlic croutons (optional; see page 81)

In a heavy-bottomed, 6-quart pot, heat olive oil over medium heat. Sauté onions, green pepper, and eggplant. Stir to brown all sides of eggplant. When onions are tender and translucent, add tomato puree and water.

Bring to a boil, then cover and simmer 20 minutes, or until puree is a dark red color.

Add carrots, celery, parsley, fresh garlic, oregano, basil, rosemary, granulated garlic, and vinegar, and simmer until carrots are just tender.

Add squash and tamari, and simmer, covered until squash is just tender.

Add salt and honey if desired. Remove from heat and serve garnished with any of the optional ingredients.

La Fiesta

Terry Shields

Cooking time: 1 hr., 20 min.   Makes 3–3½ qts.

This soup is named for a Mexican meal that Terry had eaten at a restaurant the night before. He tried to include all the ingredients from his dinner in the soup, including the guacamole. The avocado gives an unusually smooth and creamy quality. Just make sure not to heat the soup once the avocado has been added, as too much heat can spoil its delicate flavor.

½ c. pinto beans, presoaked
¼ c. kidney beans, presoaked
8 c. water
1 c. long grain brown rice
1½ c. diced yellow onion
½ c. chopped green pepper
1 Tbsp. chili powder
1 Tbsp. crumbled oregano leaf
1 1-lb. can stewed or diced
  tomatoes, blended in blender
  until smooth

3 med. cloves garlic, pressed
¼ c. minced fresh parsley
4 Tbsp. butter
⅓ c. sliced green onions (bulbs
  and tops)
2 oz. thin corn chips, preferably
  tamari-flavored
¾ c. sour cream
¼ lb. grated mild Cheddar cheese
⅓ c. peeled mashed avocado
1 tsp. Vege-Sal

Soak pinto and kidney beans in 4 cups water overnight or for at least 6 hours. Drain and discard soaking water.

In a 5- or 6-quart pot, bring to a boil: presoaked beans and 8 cups water. Reduce heat and simmer, covered, about 15 minutes. Add rice, onion, green pepper, chili powder, and oregano, and bring to second boil. Reduce heat and simmer, covered, for 40 minutes, or until rice and beans are tender. (Kidney beans take slightly longer to cook than pintos, so be sure they are tender before going to next step.)

Add blended tomatoes, garlic, parsley, and butter, and simmer 10–15 minutes, or until flavors are well blended. Stir occasionally. Turn burner to lowest heat.

Add green onions and corn chips.

In blender, blend together sour cream, Cheddar cheese, avocado, and enough of the hot soup broth so that mixture can blend. (Make sure blender cover is on tight!) Blend until smooth. Remove soup from heat; stir in blended mixture. Season with Vege-Sal, and adjust seasonings to taste. Serve, topped with additional sliced green onions, if desired.

The Lima Ohio Bean Special

Terry Shields

Cooking time: $1\frac{1}{4}$ hrs.   Makes $3\frac{1}{2}$ qts.

Terry hails from Ohio, hence the name for this lima bean soup. The Swiss cheese, mustard, lemon juice, and bean sprouts contribute to its unique flavor.

3 c. lg. dried lima beans,
  presoaked
4 bay leaves
8 c. water
2 c. (1 lg.) diced yellow onion
4 Tbsp. butter
3 c. ($\frac{1}{2}$ lb.) sliced mushrooms
$\frac{1}{3}$ c. minced fresh parsley
$1\frac{1}{2}$ tsp. crumbled oregano leaf
$\frac{1}{4}$ lb. Swiss cheese, grated
  (1 c., packed)
1 10-oz. pkg. frozen peas, rinsed
  under hot water to thaw, or
  2 c. shelled fresh peas, lightly
  steamed until tender and
  bright green

2 c. ($\frac{1}{2}$ lb.) fresh mung bean
  sprouts, chopped into 2"
  lengths
2 Tbsp. tamari
1 Tbsp. celery salt, or to taste
2 tsp. granulated garlic
2 tsp. granulated onion
$\frac{1}{2}$ tsp. prepared mustard
2 tsp. or more fresh lemon juice,
  to taste

Soak lima beans in 8 cups water for 6 hours or overnight. Drain, and discard soaking water. In a 5- or 6-quart pot, bring to a boil: presoaked beans, bay leaves, 8 cups water, and onion. Reduce heat to simmer, and cook, covered, about 40 minutes, or until beans are tender.

Add butter, mushrooms, parsley, and oregano. Continue simmering, covered, stirring occasionally, about 15 minutes more, or until beans are quite soft and have begun to form a slightly thickened broth. Remove from heat.

In blender, blend 3 cups of the hot soup (including

broth, beans, onions, and mushrooms) with the Swiss cheese, until smooth. (If it's too thick, add a little water to ease blending.) Add this mixture to the soup. Add also peas, bean sprouts, tamari, celery salt, granulated garlic, granulated onion, and mustard. Add lemon juice (see *Note*), to taste. Soup should be of medium thickness; add additional water, if necessary. Heat at very low setting, without boiling, stirring often, just until hot. Serve.

Note: The addition of lemon juice to this soup serves to lighten the flavor without giving it a real lemony taste. Lemons, however, vary a lot in flavor and strength, so 2 teaspoons is only a rough estimate of how much to add. (Once when making this recipe, I needed 8 teaspoons of lemon juice to get the right flavor, because that particular lemon was very mild.) Add a little at a time and taste as you go, and stop before it's too lemony. When the soup tastes lighter and snappier, that's it.

Macaroni and Cheese Soup

Paul Lewin
Janice Cook Migliaccio

Cooking time: 1½ hrs.   Makes 3½ qts.

Vegetables and spices in a creamy base give pizzazz to this variation of a classic casserole. Variations include Mom's Macaroni and Cheese and Paul's Macaroni and Cheese.

6 c. water
1 lg. (⅓ lb.) grated summer squash, the pale green, flying saucer type
1 c. diced green cabbage
1 med. diced yellow onion
1 c. (2 med.) diced carrots
¼ c. diced green pepper
2 lg. cloves garlic, pressed
1 sm. bay leaf
2 tsp. onion powder
¼ tsp. granulated garlic
1 pt. half and half

8 oz. grated Cheddar cheese
4 oz. grated jack cheese
1 lb. pasta shells or macaroni, cooked until just tender (al dente)—use medium-sized whole grain shells or Vegeroni or bow ties, or a combination (Vegeroni provides great color, and the different textures look interesting and delicious)
dash of cayenne, to taste
Vege-Sal or sea salt to taste

In a 5-quart pot, bring to a boil: water, summer squash, cabbage, onion, carrots, green pepper, fresh garlic, and bay leaf. Cover tightly and simmer about 1 hour, or until vegetables are very tender.

Meanwhile, cook pasta according to package directions, until just tender; rinse, drain, and set aside, covered.

Pour soup broth and vegetables into a blender (you may have to do this in two batches). Add onion powder and granulated garlic, and blend until smooth. Pour mixture back into soup pot, and heat gently. When quite hot, but not boiling, add half and half and grated cheese. Heat at lowest setting—it's important to keep the soup from boiling (cheese may curdle if it does). When soup is quite hot, add cooked pasta. Continue heating gently, 5–10 minutes.

Remove from heat. Add cayenne and Vege-Sal or sea salt, to taste. Cover and let sit 10 minutes. (The pasta will expand slightly and absorb flavor from the soup. Don't let it sit any longer, however, or the soup may turn into a casserole as the pasta keeps expanding.) Adjust seasonings if necessary. Serve.

Variation: Mom's Macaroni and Cheese Soup

Add, along with pasta:

1 16-oz. can whole peeled tomatoes, chopped into small pieces (reserve liquid for stock in another soup, or add to this recipe, making a thinner, tomatoey soup)
1 tsp. bakon flavored yeast (mix yeast with small amount of soup broth or water until a smooth paste forms, without lumps; stir into soup)

Variation: Paul's Macaroni and Cheese Soup

Instead of blending all the broth and vegetables together, blend only half of the vegetables. This gives the soup a nice, slightly chunky texture.

Mac's Navy Bean

Kristine Molasky-McCallister

Cooking time: 1 hr., 20 min.   Makes 4 qts.

A flavorful and quite attractive mixture of beans, vegetables, and seasonings.

$3\frac{1}{4}$ c. navy beans, presoaked
8 c. water
2 Tbsp. diced green pepper
2 c. chopped yellow onion
3 c. diced celery
$\frac{1}{4}$ c. tamari
2 Tbsp. nutritional yeast flakes
3 cloves garlic, pressed or minced
$\frac{3}{4}$ tsp. ground caraway seed
$\frac{1}{2}$ tsp. ground sage
1 16-oz. can tomatoes, diced
   (include juice)
1 c. diced carrot

1 med. leek, thinly sliced (both
   white and green parts)
1 c. shredded green cabbage
dash of cayenne or black pepper,
   to taste
sea salt to taste
3 Tbsp. (or less) additional
   tamari, to taste
$\frac{1}{2}$ tsp. additional ground caraway,
   or to taste
$\frac{1}{4}$ tsp. additional ground sage, or
   to taste

Soak beans in 6 cups water overnight or for at least 6 hours. Drain and discard soaking water.

In a 5- or 6-quart pot, bring to a boil: 8 cups water, presoaked beans, green pepper, onion, celery, tamari, yeast flakes, garlic, caraway, and sage. Simmer, covered, stirring occasionally, for about 1 hour, or until beans are quite tender.

Add tomatoes, carrot, leek, and cabbage. Simmer until added vegetables are tender, about 10–15 minutes. Season with pepper, salt, and additional tamari, caraway, and sage to taste. Serve.

Minestrone

Marsha Stamp

Cooking time: 1¼ hrs.   Makes 4½–5 qts.

Our vegetarian version of this classic Italian soup. Serve with garlic bread and top with grated Parmesan cheese to complete the meal.

4 c. water—reserve 2 c. to adjust thickness later

3 qts. fresh tomato puree—5½ lbs. (18 med.) ripe tomatoes, blended in blender

⅓ c. unrefined olive oil

4 c. thinly sliced celery (include finely diced leaves)

2 c. chopped red onion

1½ tsp. cut thyme leaf

6 bay leaves

2 c. eggplant (unpeeled), chopped into small cubes

1½ c. carrots, quartered lengthwise, then sliced ¼" thick

3 Tbsp. crumbled oregano

1 Tbsp. dried parsley, crumbled

2 Tbsp. crumbled basil

6 med. cloves garlic, pressed or minced

5 c. (2 lbs.) zucchini, sliced in thick rounds or chopped into cubes

4 c. broccoli—thinly sliced stalks; bite-sized flowerettes

⅓ c. tamari

2 tsp. apple cider vinegar

1–2 Tbsp. honey, to taste

2–2½ c. cooked garbanzo beans* (¾ c. dry)

2 tsp. Spike

2 tsp. sea salt or Vege-Sal, or to taste

6 oz. whole wheat shells or elbow macaroni, cooked al dente (until just tender)

Bring to a boil: 2 cups water, tomato puree, olive oil, celery, onion, thyme, and bay leaves. Simmer, covered, ½ hour.

Add eggplant, carrots, oregano, parsley, basil, and garlic, and simmer, covered, 15 minutes, stirring occasionally.

Add zucchini and broccoli and simmer 10 or 15 minutes, or until tender. Stir occasionally.

Add tamari, vinegar, honey, garbanzos, Spike, and salt. Add water if a thinner soup is desired. Adjust seasonings to taste. Add macaroni or shells, and simmer over low heat for about 10 minutes, stirring occasionally, until nice and hot. Serve.

Note: The taste of fresh tomatoes is important to this soup. If fresh tomatoes are out of season, however, you can make puree by blending canned whole or chopped tomatoes in blender to make 3 quarts.

*To Cook Garbanzo Beans

Soak beans for 6 hours or overnight in plenty of cold water. Drain off soaking water. Place beans in a saucepan, with fresh water to cover. Bring to a boil; add 1 teaspoon salt. (Adding salt at this point usually keeps the skins from coming off the beans, thus they are more attractive.) Lower heat and simmer, covered, about $1-1\frac{1}{2}$ hours, or until tender. Check water level occasionally and add more if necessary. During last 15 minutes of cooking add 2 tablespoons tamari (or salt, to taste), to make beans more flavorful. The tamari also gives the beans a nice color.

Miso Vegetable

Janice Cook Migliaccio

Easy
Cooking time: 45 min.   Makes 3½ qts.

This traditional Japanese-style soup is simple, quick to pre-pare, and gets its full-bodied flavor from miso paste. You may substitute other fresh vegetables in season.

2 Tbsp. sesame or safflower oil
1 c. (1 med.) yellow onion, cut in thin half-circles
1½ c. (3 lg. stalks) celery, sliced diagonally
1½ c. (2 lg.) carrots, sliced diagonally, ¼" thick
8 c. water
3 c. thinly sliced green cabbage (or Chinese cabbage)
2 c. chopped kale or bok choy leaves (optional)

juice of 1 tsp. freshly grated ginger*
4–6 Tbsp. miso (brown rice or barley miso is nice; you may use others, or even a combination for a full flavor)
1 10-oz. pkg. tofu, cubed (optional)
2 Tbsp. sliced green onions, as garnish
tamari or sea salt, to taste

In a heavy-bottomed, 5- or 6-quart pot, gently heat 2 tablespoons oil. Add onions and celery and sauté, stirring often, until lightly browned, about 10 minutes. Add carrots and continue sautéing 5–10 minutes more, stirring to brown carrots.

Add water and bring to a boil; reduce heat to low and simmer gently, uncovered, until carrots are just tender, about 10–15 minutes.

Add cabbage, kale or bok choy, and ginger juice. Simmer 5–10 minutes longer, or until cabbage is tender. Turn off heat.

In a small bowl, combine miso with enough of the hot soup broth to make a thin paste. Stir into soup.

Gently stir in tofu chunks, if desired. Add tamari or sea salt, to taste. Serve garnished with chopped green onions.

*Ginger Juice

Finely grate a small piece of ginger until you have about 1 teaspoon. Place in a garlic press or in the palm of your hand, and squeeze tightly, catching the juice in a container.

Mushroom Barley Cauliflower

Marsha Stamp

Cooking time: $1\frac{1}{4}$ hrs.   Makes 4 qts.

This soup is one of Follow Your Heart's most popular. Many variations of it exist, and you're welcome to discover your own. It's quite hearty.

8 c. water
$5\frac{1}{2}$ c. (1 lb.) sliced mushrooms
2 c. (1 med.) chopped yellow
  onion
2 c. chopped celery
$\frac{3}{4}$ c. ($\frac{1}{3}$ lb.) hulled or pearl barley
4 Tbsp. butter
$\frac{1}{4}$ c. tamari
1 Tbsp. granulated garlic
4 tsp. crumbled basil
1 lg. head cauliflower—$\frac{3}{4}$ c. diced
  stem and core; 3 c. bite-sized
  flowerettes

2 c. (1 med.) cubed ($\frac{1}{2}''$) russet
  potato (unpeeled)
$\frac{3}{4}$ c. (1 lg.) carrot, quartered
  lengthwise, then diced
1 10-oz. pkg. frozen peas, rinsed
  under hot water to thaw, or
  2 c. shelled fresh peas
2–3 Tbsp. fresh lemon juice, to
  taste

In a 5- or 6-quart pot, bring to a boil: water, mushrooms, onion, celery, barley, butter, and tamari. Reduce heat; add garlic and basil. Simmer, covered, about 30 minutes, or until barley is slightly tender. Stir occasionally.

To prepare cauliflower, quarter head, then dice stem and core and break flowerettes into bite-sized pieces.

Add diced cauliflower stem, potato, and carrot. Again bring to a boil, then reduce heat and continue simmering, covered, until barley and vegetables are quite tender, about 15 minutes.

Add cauliflowerettes. Simmer 10–15 minutes, or until flowerettes are just tender.

Reduce to lowest heat. Add peas and lemon juice and heat gently a few minutes, until peas are bright green. Adjust seasonings to taste. Serve.

Mushroom Stroganoff Soup

Micki Besancon

Cooking time: 45 min.   Makes 4 qts.

Without a doubt, this is the richest tasting soup we offer. Customers clamor for it. Serve with a salad.

6 c. water
5½–6 c. (3 med.) diced russet potatoes (unpeeled)
1½ c. diced yellow onion—reserve ½ c.
¼ c. Jensen's broth powder
4 Tbsp. butter
6 c. (1 lb.) sliced mushrooms
¼ c. tamari
2 Tbsp. Spike
1 Tbsp. sweet basil
1 Tbsp. dried parsley flakes
1 Tbsp. granulated garlic
2 tsp. whole celery seed

8 oz. cream cheese
4 oz. shredded sharp Cheddar cheese
1 oz. (2 Tbsp.) crumbled blue cheese
2 c. (1 pt.) sour cream
1 c. milk
1 c. shelled fresh peas, lightly steamed until tender and bright green (or frozen peas, rinsed in hot water to thaw)
8 oz. whole wheat ribbon noodles, cooked al dente (just tender), rinsed, and drained

In a 5- or 6-quart pot, combine water, potatoes, 1 cup onions, and Jensen's broth powder. Bring to a boil. Cook covered (medium heat) about 20 minutes, or until potatoes begin to dissolve and form a broth. Stir occasionally.

Meanwhile, in a large skillet sauté the reserved ½ cup onions with the mushrooms in butter until onions are tender and mushrooms reduced in size. (Skillet should still have a little mushroom juice in it, brought out by the cooking.) Add tamari, Spike, basil, parsley, garlic, and celery seed to mushroom mixture, and sauté for another 2 minutes. Add this mixture to the soup base.

In blender, blend cheeses, sour cream, and milk until smooth, and add to the soup base. Add peas and noodles and heat gently, stirring often, until peas are tender and all is hot. (Careful not to boil it, though, or milk will curdle.) Garnish with fresh parsley, if desired. Serve.

Old Fashioned Stew

Marsha Stamp

Easy
Cooking time: 1 hr.   Makes 5 qts.

Resembles a basic beef stew, without the beef! Textured vegeta-ble protein is a dry soybean-based product which makes a deli-cious substitute for meat. If it is unavailable in your area, you may simply omit the textured vegetable protein and you'll still have a good vegetable stew. Or substitute a wheat product called "wheat-meat," or wheat gluten.

8 c. water
$2\frac{1}{2}$ c. (2 med.) diced yellow onion
3 c. (4 lg. stalks) chopped celery
2 c. dry textured vegetable pro-tein, $\frac{1}{2}$–$\frac{3}{4}$" chunks
$\frac{3}{4}$ tsp. crumbled basil leaf
2 lg. cloves garlic, pressed or minced
$\frac{1}{4}$ c. tamari

4 c. carrots, sliced in $\frac{1}{2}$" rounds
8 c. (3 lg.) russet potatoes (un-peeled), cut into 1" squares
1 c. shelled fresh peas, or frozen peas rinsed under hot water to thaw
2 Tbsp. brown rice flour, whisked into $\frac{1}{2}$ c. cool water

In a 6-quart pot, bring to a boil: water, onion, celery, and textured vegetable protein. Reduce heat to medium and cook, covered, until textured vegetable protein is ten-der, about 15 minutes.

Add basil, garlic, tamari, and carrots. Simmer, covered, stirring occasionally, until carrots are slightly tender (about 15 minutes).

Add potatoes and simmer, covered, stirring occasion-ally, until potatoes are tender but still intact, about 10–15 minutes. Add peas and reduce to lowest heat.

Whisk brown rice flour into $\frac{1}{2}$ cup cool water, until smooth. Gently but quickly stir this mixture into the soup, and continue simmering, on low heat, until soup thickens (about 5 minutes). Add additional tamari to taste. Serve.

Oriental Vegetable

Hedy Kelho

Easy
Cooking time: 30 min.   Makes $3\frac{1}{2}$ qts.

A light vegetable soup with Oriental seasonings.

3 Tbsp. sesame or safflower oil
2 c. (2 med.) carrots, cut diagonally $\frac{1}{4}''$ thick
$1\frac{1}{2}$ c. (3 lg. stalks) celery, cut on diagonal $\frac{1}{2}''$ thick
1 Tbsp. dried, crumbled hijiki or arame seaweed (optional)
2 c. (1 med.) yellow onion, cut in thin half-circles
$1\frac{1}{2}$ c. ($\frac{1}{4}$ lb.) mushrooms, sliced $\frac{1}{4}''$ thick
$\frac{1}{2}$ c. raw cashew pieces or whole cashews
8 c. water
1–3 tsp. fresh ginger juice*

1 c. (1–2 sm. cans) sliced water chestnuts
1 c. ($\frac{1}{4}$ lb.) fresh Chinese snow peas or sugar-snap peas (if fresh are unavailable, substitute frozen and be careful not to overcook)
1 10-oz. pkg. tofu, cut into 1″ × 1″ cubes, and baked or pan fried until crisp** (optional)
2 c. ($\frac{1}{4}$ lb.) fresh mung bean sprouts
4–6 Tbsp. tamari

Heat oil over a medium heat in a heavy-bottomed 5- or 6-quart pot. Add and sauté: carrots, celery, seaweed (see *Note*), onions, mushrooms, and cashews. Stir often to brown vegetables evenly. When they are slightly tender, and still a little crisp, add water and ginger juice. Bring to a boil; reduce heat to simmer and cook about 10 minutes.

Turn burner to lowest heat. Add water chestnuts and snow peas or sugar-snap peas, and simmer 5 minutes. Turn off heat. Add tofu, bean sprouts, and tamari to taste. Adjust seasonings (check ginger). Serve immediately.

Note: Seaweed has a strong flavor, reminiscent of the ocean, and it is high in certain minerals. Many enjoy the taste, but to some it is fishy. If you're in doubt but still want to try it, start with a lesser amount.

*Ginger Juice

Finely grate a 2″ × 3″ piece of fresh ginger root. Place in a garlic press or squeeze tightly in palm of your hand, catching the juice in a cup; the garlic press works most efficiently. Fresh ginger varies greatly in strength and spiciness, so add a teaspoon at a time until desired gingeriness is reached. Keep in mind that the broth will taste pretty bland until the tamari is added. Tamari will nicely compliment the ginger flavor.

**To Bake Tofu

Place cubes on a lightly oiled pan and bake in a preheated 400° oven for a few minutes. When edges start to brown, flip cubes over and brown other sides until tofu is firm and slightly crisp. (Removing the moisture from the tofu in this way keeps the cubes from breaking apart in the soup.)

An alternate method: Dry the cubes by patting gently between cloth or paper towels. Heat a little butter or oil in a skillet; add tofu, and fry until crisp, turning gently to brown all sides. Drain on paper towels to remove any excess oil.

Pablo's Creamy Corn

Erley Lawrence

Cooking time: 1 hr., 20 min.   Makes 4½ qts.

Mexican-style seasonings in an unusual, creamy soup.

⅔ c. (¼ lb.) pinto beans, presoaked
7 c. water
1 Tbsp. olive oil
¼ c. tamari
1½ c. diced yellow onion
1½ c. diced celery
3 med. cloves garlic, pressed
2 Tbsp. cumin
2 Tbsp. chili powder
2 tsp. granulated onion
1 tsp. crumbled oregano leaf
½ tsp. crumbled basil leaf
3 c. (2 med.) yellow squash, sliced in thin rounds

1½ c. (1 med.) zucchini, sliced in thin rounds
3 c. fresh or frozen corn (if frozen, rinse under hot water to thaw)
½ c. fresh or frozen peas (if frozen, rinse under hot water to thaw)
4 corn tortillas, cut in wedges
1 c. shredded red cabbage
4 Tbsp. butter
¾ c. tahini (raw sesame butter)
1 c. sour cream
Vege-Sal to taste (optional)

Soak pinto beans in 2 cups water for 6 hours or overnight. Drain and discard soaking water.

In a 5- or 6-quart pot, bring to a boil: water, presoaked beans, olive oil, tamari, and onion. Reduce heat and simmer, covered, for about ½ hour, or until beans are slightly tender.

Add celery, garlic, cumin, chili powder, granulated onion, oregano, and basil, and continue simmering until beans are tender, about 30 minutes.

Add yellow squash, zucchini, corn, peas, tortillas, and red cabbage. Simmer 10–15 minutes, or until added veggies are just tender.

Turn burner to lowest heat. Add butter. Blend tahini and sour cream in blender with enough hot soup broth to make a thick cream, about $1\frac{1}{2}$ cups of broth. (Make sure blender cover is on tight!) Blend until smooth, then stir mixture into soup.

Add Vege-Sal if desired, and adjust seasonings to taste. Serve.

Pappy's Black Bean

Marsha Stamp

Easy
Cooking time: 1–1¼ hrs.   Makes 4 qts.

Serve this hearty, slightly sweet soup with corn bread and a dark green salad.

3 c. (1¼ lbs.) black beans,
  presoaked
8 c. water
2 c. (2 sm.) diced yellow onion
2 c. (3 lg. stalks) sliced celery
1 c. (1 lg.) carrot, quartered
  lengthwise, then sliced ¼" thick
1½ c. (1 lg.) yam, halved
  lengthwise, then sliced ¼" thick
1 Tbsp. crumbled basil
2 tsp. crumbled oregano

2 tsp. granulated garlic, or 3 lg.
  cloves fresh garlic, pressed or
  minced
½ tsp. bakon bits, or ½–1 tsp.
  bakon flavored yeast
2 Tbsp. Barbados or other light
  molasses (or pure maple
  syrup), or to taste
1 tsp. apple cider vinegar
¼ c. tamari
sea salt to taste

Soak beans for 8 hours or overnight. Drain; discard soaking water. Bring beans and 8 cups water to a boil. Simmer, covered, 20 minutes to ½ hour, or until beans are slightly tender.

Add onions, celery, and carrots. Bring to a simmer, and cook until vegetables are tender, about 10–15 minutes.

Add yams, basil, oregano, and garlic, and simmer until yams are barely tender, about 15 minutes.

Turn burner to lowest heat. Ladle about ¾ cup of the hot soup broth into blender container with bakon bits or bakon yeast; blend until smooth. Add to soup, along with molasses, vinegar, and tamari. Heat at low setting, stirring often. Season with sea salt, to taste. Serve.

Popeye's Swee'pea with Olive Oyl

Marsha Stamp

Cooking time: 1¼ hrs.   Makes 4½–5 qts.

This soup contains all of Popeye's favorites—peas sweetened with yams ("I yam what I yam"), olive oil, and, of course, spinach.

10 c. water
3¼ c. (1½ lbs.) dried green split peas
2 c. (1 lg.) diced red onion
2 c. (½ lb.) diced yam (unpeeled)
2 c. (3 lg. stalks) chopped celery (include finely diced leaves)
3 Tbsp. unrefined olive oil
1 lb. finely chopped fresh spinach (wash well—see "Washing, Soaking, and Cleaning" section)

2 lg. cloves garlic, pressed or minced
2 tsp. crumbled basil leaf
2 c. shelled fresh peas, or 1 10-oz. pkg. frozen peas, rinsed under hot water to thaw
3 Tbsp. tamari
3 Tbsp. Barbados or other light molasses, or to taste (do not use blackstrap)
2 tsp. Spike, or to taste

In a 6- or 8-quart pot, bring to a boil: water, split peas, onion, yam, celery, and olive oil. Reduce heat and simmer, covered, about 30 minutes.

Add spinach, garlic, and basil. Bring again to a boil; reduce heat and simmer, covered, about 25–35 minutes,

or until split peas have dissolved to form a thick broth. Stir occasionally.

Add fresh or frozen peas and tamari. Add molasses and Spike, to taste, and simmer 5 minutes, until peas are tender and flavors well blended. Serve.

Pumpkin Pie Soup

Bob Goldberg
Janice Cook Migliaccio
Paul Lewin

Easy
Cooking time: 40 min.   Makes $2\frac{1}{2}$ qts.

Serve this at the beginning of a fall or winter meal, or even as dessert. It's slightly sweet, and you can adjust the sweetness to your liking.

4 c. water
1 c. diced yellow onion
1 c. diced carrot
3 c. pumpkin puree (fresh cooked
  pumpkin or 1 29-oz. can)
$\frac{1}{2}$ tsp. cinnamon
$\frac{1}{4}$ tsp. nutmeg
$\frac{1}{4}$ tsp. allspice

$\frac{1}{4}$ tsp. sea salt, or to taste
$\frac{1}{8}$ tsp. cloves
$\frac{1}{8}$ tsp. ginger
2 Tbsp. butter
$\frac{1}{4}$ c. cream
$\frac{1}{4}$ c. Barbados or other light
  molasses (not blackstrap)
$\frac{1}{4}$ c. honey, or to taste

In a 4- or 5-quart pot, bring to a boil: water, onion, and carrot. Reduce heat and simmer, covered, until carrots and onion are very tender, about 20 minutes.

Add pumpkin puree, spices, and butter. Simmer gently a few minutes, stirring occasionally, until puree is very hot. (Add more water here if necessary.)

Turn burner to lowest heat. Add cream, molasses, and honey. (Pumpkin varies in sweetness, so add honey a little at a time, and adjust to taste.) Adjust other seasonings to taste. Serve, garnished with a dollop of whipped cream, if desired.

Rainbow Vegetable

Bonnie Chappell McKelligott

Cooking time: $1\frac{1}{4}$ hrs.   Makes $4\frac{1}{2}$ qts.

A colorful array of garden vegetables. You may use different vegetables in season, keeping in mind a balance of colors, and cooking so that they remain firm and brightly colored.

8 c. water
1 c. diced yellow onion
$\frac{3}{4}$ c. sliced celery
3 Tbsp. diced green or red pepper
$1\frac{1}{2}$ tsp. thyme leaf, cut (not ground)
1 c. carrot, sliced in rounds
1 c. russet potato (unpeeled), chopped into small chunks
2 med. cloves garlic, pressed or minced
$\frac{1}{2}$ tsp. crumbled basil leaf
$\frac{1}{2}$ tsp. crumbled oregano leaf
$\frac{1}{2}$ tsp. ground celery seed
1 lb. cauliflower—1 c. finely diced stem and core; 2 c. bite-sized flowerettes
$\frac{3}{4}$ lb. broccoli—$1\frac{1}{2}$ c. finely diced stem; 2 c. bite-sized flowerettes

1 c. sliced yellow squash or zucchini
1 c. finely chopped fresh spinach, kale, or swiss chard
1 c. corn, fresh or frozen (if frozen, rinse under hot water to thaw)
1 c. peas, fresh or frozen (if frozen, rinse under hot water to thaw)
$1\frac{1}{2}$ c. diced fresh tomato
2 Tbsp. minced fresh parsley
$1\frac{1}{2}$ c. shredded red cabbage
$\frac{1}{4}$ c. tamari
2 Tbsp. sesame seeds (optional)
2 Tbsp. nutritional yeast flakes
1 tsp. granulated onion

In a 5- or 6-quart pot, bring to a boil: water, diced onion, celery, pepper, and thyme. Reduce heat and simmer, covered, about $\frac{1}{2}$ hour (make sure soup is bubbling slightly).

Add carrot, potato, garlic, basil, oregano, and celery seed, and simmer, covered, about 20 minutes, or until carrot and potato are a little tender.

To prepare cauliflower and broccoli, first discard woody

stem, then slice remaining stem (or core) and break flowerettes into bite-sized pieces.

Add cauliflower, broccoli, squash, spinach, corn, peas, tomatoes, and parsley. Simmer 5 minutes.

Add red cabbage, and simmer 5 minutes more, or until cauliflower is just tender.

Add tamari, sesame seeds, yeast, and granulated onion. Simmer 5 minutes, or until flavors are well blended. Adjust seasonings to taste.

Serve immediately. This soup is best when served fresh, because the rainbow colors are most brilliant. It tastes great when reheated, but the colors will be subdued.

Spaghetti Soup

Micki Besancon
Bonnie Chappell McKelligott
Hedy Kelho

Cooking time: 1 hr.   Makes 3–3½ qts.

Spaghetti lovers will appreciate this one.

2 c. water
6 c. tomato puree (3 1-lb. cans
    diced or whole tomatoes,
    blended in blender until
    smooth)
2 lg. bay leaves
2 Tbsp. unrefined olive oil
2 c. chopped yellow onion
1½ c. finely chopped celery
¼ c. diced red or green pepper
1 Tbsp. crumbled oregano
4 med. cloves garlic, pressed or
    minced
1 tsp. crumbled basil
1½ c. (1 med.) zucchini, cut in
    thin half-circles
1¼ c. (1 med.) yellow squash, cut
    in thin half-circles

3 c. (2 lg.) finely chopped fresh
    tomato (unpeeled)
4 oz. whole wheat or wheat-soy
    spaghetti, broken in half,
    cooked al dente (just tender)
2 Tbsp. nutritional yeast
    (optional)
1 Tbsp. tamari
1–2 tsp. honey, to taste
1 tsp. apple cider vinegar
½ tsp. garlic powder
sea salt to taste
4 oz. grated Cheddar (blended
    with a little hot soup broth) or
    ¼ c. grated Parmesan cheese
    (stirred into hot soup)—
    (optional)

In a 5- or 6-quart pot, bring to a boil: water, tomato puree, and bay leaves. Reduce heat and simmer about 20 minutes, until bay leaves are fragrant. Meanwhile, heat olive oil in a large skillet. Add and sauté the onion, celery, and pepper until vegetables are slightly browned and a little tender, about 15 minutes.

To the simmering tomato puree, add the sautéed veggies along with the oregano, fresh garlic, basil, zucchini, yellow squash, and fresh tomato. Simmer until veggies are just tender, about 15 minutes. (Meanwhile, cook spaghetti, according to package directions, until just tender.)

Reduce to lowest heat. Season with nutritional yeast, tamari, honey, vinegar, garlic powder, and sea salt. Stir in cooked spaghetti. Adjust seasonings to taste. Serve as is, or you may add Cheddar or Parmesan cheese.

Spencer's Chili

Spencer Windbiel

Cooking time: 1¼ hrs.   Makes 4 qts.

Real hearty, this soup is spicy, with the flavor of jalapeno peppers. Add as much or as little spiciness as you like.

1½ c. (⅔ lb.) pinto beans,
  presoaked
1 c. (⅓ lb.) kidney beans,
  presoaked
8 c. water
1½ Tbsp. unrefined olive oil
1 lg. bay leaf
½ c. lentils, dry
⅔ c. (1 sm. chopped green
  pepper
1 c. (1 med.) carrot, sliced into
  ¼″ rounds
2 c. (1 med.) diced yellow onion
2 c. (1 lg.) fresh tomato, chopped,
  or 1 16-oz. can whole peeled
  tomatoes, chopped (reserve
  liquid; add if soup is too thick)
2 Tbsp. chili powder

1 Tbsp. ground cumin
1½ tsp. granulated garlic
1 tsp. crumbled basil
½ tsp. crumbled oregano leaf
¼ tsp. cut thyme leaf
3 Tbsp. dried chives
1½ c. corn kernels, fresh or frozen
  (if frozen, rinse under hot
  water to thaw)
5 corn tortillas, cut in wedges
1 8-oz. can tomato sauce
  (Spanish-style, or regular)
1 fresh jalapeno chili pepper
1 Tbsp. Spike
2–4 Tbsp. tamari
sea salt to taste
⅓ c. sliced green onions

Soak pinto and kidney beans in 6 cups water for 6 hours or overnight. Drain and discard soaking liquid.

In a 5- or 6-quart pot, bring to a boil: presoaked pinto and kidney beans, 8 cups water, olive oil, bay leaf, and lentils. Reduce heat and simmer, covered, until beans are slightly tender (about ½ hour).

Add green pepper, carrot, onion, fresh tomato (or use canned tomatoes instead at next step), chili powder, cumin, garlic, basil, oregano, and thyme. Cover and continue simmering, stirring occasionally, until beans are very tender, about another ½ hour.

Add chives, corn, corn tortillas, tomato sauce, and canned tomatoes (omit if using fresh). Add reserved tomato liquid or a little water if soup is too thick. Turn burner to lowest heat and continue heating, covered.

Meanwhile, place the jalapeno pepper in a small unoiled pan and roast in a 400° oven until the skin has turned light brown and bubbles a little. Rinse under cold water; remove stem.

In a blender container, place 1 cup of the already prepared hot soup (try to use mostly broth and avoid the beans). Cut jalapeno pepper into quarters, add $\frac{1}{4}$ of the chili to soup in blender, and blend until smooth. Add to soup, along with the Spike, tamari, and sea salt.

Give it a taste. If you'd like it hotter, blend more jalapeno pepper into the soup until the desired spiciness is reached. Serve garnished with green onion.

Note: Jalapeno peppers vary in hotness—$\frac{1}{4}$ of a pepper may be plenty this time but next time you may need a whole one. Also, if fresh jalapeno chilies are unavailable, you may substitute 4 ounces of canned green chilies, blended in a blender until smooth, with a dash of cayenne pepper. This is only an emergency measure, however; fresh jalapeno peppers really do taste the best.

Split Pea Soup

Michael Besancon
Spencer Windbiel

Easy
Cooking time: $1\frac{1}{4}$ hrs.   Makes $3\frac{1}{2}$–4 qts.

A very basic and simply delicious split pea vegetable soup.

8 c. water
2 c. dried green split peas
3 c. (3 lg. stalks) chopped celery
2 c. (1 lg.) chopped onion
2 tsp. cut thyme leaf
2 lg. bay leaves
2 c. (2 med.) carrots, cut in
$\frac{1}{2}$" rounds
2 lg. cloves garlic, pressed or
minced
1 tsp. crumbled basil leaf
$\frac{1}{2}$ tsp. oregano
2–$2\frac{1}{2}$ c. (1 lg.) chopped russet
potato

$\frac{1}{4}$ c. green onions, finely chopped
1 Tbsp. Spike
1 Tbsp. tamari (optional)
sea salt to taste
pinch of cayenne pepper
(optional)
2 Tbsp. butter or olive oil
(optional)
2 c. shelled fresh peas, or 1 10-oz.
pkg. frozen peas, rinsed under
hot water to thaw (optional)

In a 5- or 6-quart pot, bring to a boil: water, split peas, celery, onion, thyme, and bay leaves. Reduce heat and simmer, covered, about 20 minutes, or until split peas are a little soft.

Add carrots, garlic, basil, and oregano; bring to a second boil, then continue simmering, covered, until split peas are very tender and are dissolving to form a thick broth.

Add potato, and simmer until potato is tender but still firm.

Turn burner to lowest heat. Add green onions, Spike, tamari, sea salt, and cayenne pepper to taste.

Add butter or olive oil, and peas, if desired. Heat gently, stirring, until fresh or frozen peas are tender. Serve.

Sweet and Sour Oriental Vegetable

Janice Cook Migliaccio

Cooking time: 1 hr.   Makes 4½–5 qts.

This tasty soup was originally created from the leftovers of a sweet and sour vegetable dinner.

2 Tbsp. sesame or safflower oil

2 c. (2 med.) yellow onion, cut in thin half-circles

2 c. (3–4 lg. stalks) thinly sliced celery, cut diagonally

1 c. (1 lg.) green pepper, chopped into ½" squares

¾ c. long grain brown rice

6 c. water

2 c. pineapple juice (if using canned pineapple [below], use that juice for part of the 2 c.)

1½ c. (2–3 med.) thinly sliced carrot, cut diagonally

1½–2 tsp. ground ginger (or fresh ginger juice*), to taste

4 med. cloves garlic, pressed

1½ c. fresh pineapple chunks, or 1 20-oz. can unsweetened pineapple chunks

1 28-oz. can whole tomatoes, diced (include juice)

1 6-oz. can tomato paste

½ c. mild honey

2–4 Tbsp. apple cider vinegar, to taste

1 c. slivered or sliced almonds

1 10-oz. pkg. tofu, drained, cut into ¾" cubes and baked**

1 sm. can sliced water chestnuts

3 c. (⅓ lb.) mung bean sprouts

¼ c. tamari, or to taste

In a heavy-bottomed, 5- or 6-quart pot, heat oil over medium heat. Add onions, celery, green pepper, and rice, and sauté until golden, stirring frequently.

Add water, pineapple juice, and carrots. Bring to a boil; reduce heat and simmer, covered, about 20 minutes, or until rice is a little tender.

Add ginger, garlic, pineapple, tomatoes, and tomato paste, and continue simmering, covered, about 20–25 minutes, or until rice is quite tender. Stir occasionally.

Turn burner to lowest heat. Add honey and apple cider vinegar, to taste. Add almonds, tofu, water chestnuts, bean sprouts, and tamari. Adjust seasonings to your liking, and serve.

**Ginger Juice*

Finely grate a 1" × 2" piece of fresh ginger. Place grated ginger in a garlic press, and squeeze the ginger juice into a container. Add to soup to taste.

***To Bake Tofu*

Place cubes on a lightly oiled pan and bake in a preheated 400° oven for a few minutes. When edges start to brown, flip cubes over and brown other sides until tofu is firm and slightly crisp. (Removing the moisture from the tofu in this way keeps the cubes from breaking apart in the soup.)

An alternate method: Dry the cubes by patting gently between cloth or paper towels. Heat a little butter or oil in a skillet; add tofu, and fry until crisp, turning gently to brown all sides. Drain on paper towels to remove any excess oil.

Tamale Soup

Spencer Windbiel
Terry Shields

Cooking time: 1 hr.   Makes 3½–4 qts.

The flavor of tamales is conveyed in this simple, nourishing soup.

2⅔ c. (1 lb.) pinto beans, presoaked
8 c. water
1 lg. bay leaf
1 c. chopped yellow onion
½ c. diced green or red pepper
2 c. chopped celery
1 Tbsp. dried chives
1 tsp. celery salt

3 med. cloves garlic, pressed or minced
1 Tbsp. tamari
¼ tsp. cayenne pepper
2 tsp. ground cumin
⅓ c. olive oil
¾ c. (¼ lb.) yellow corn meal
1 Tbsp. bakon bits
sea salt to taste

Soak beans in 6 cups water for at least 6 hours or over-night. Drain and discard soaking water.

In a 5- or 6-quart pot, bring to a boil: water, presoaked pinto beans, and bay leaf. Simmer, covered, for about 20 minutes.

Add onion, pepper, celery, chives, celery salt, garlic, tamari, cayenne, cumin, and olive oil. Bring again to a boil, then reduce heat and simmer, covered, until beans are tender, about 30 minutes.

In blender, blend 2 cups of the hot soup broth with the cornmeal and bakon bits until smooth. (Keep lid on *tight*.) Stirring constantly, add the cornmeal mixture gradually to the soup. Simmer and continue stirring, for about 10 minutes, or until cornmeal is cooked (soup will thicken). Add salt, and adjust seasonings, to taste. Serve.

Tomato Cabbage

Brion Levitsky

Easy
Cooking time: 1 hr.   Makes 3½–4 qts.

This tangy soup has a slightly sweet and sour taste. It is well loved by our customers. A colorful soup.

8 c. tomato puree—4 lbs. chopped, unpeeled ripe tomatoes (or 3 1-lb. cans whole or diced tomatoes and 2 c. water) blended until smooth
4 c. green cabbage—2 c. diced; 2 c. thinly sliced or shredded
3½ c. red cabbage—1½ c. diced; 2 c. thinly sliced or shredded
2½ c. (1 lg.) finely chopped red onion
½ tsp. cut thyme leaf
2 tsp. dill seed

3 lg. cloves garlic, pressed or minced
1 Tbsp. dill weed
½ tsp. crumbled oregano leaf
½ tsp. crumbled basil leaf
2 tsp. apple cider vinegar, or to taste
1 Tbsp. Dr. Bronner's seasoning powder
2 tsp. Spike
granulated or powdered garlic, to taste

Bring to a boil: tomato puree, diced green and red cabbage, onion, thyme, and dill seed. Reduce heat and simmer, covered, about ½ hour, or until cabbage is very soft. (If using fresh tomatoes, color will change from pink to deep red.)

Add garlic, dill weed, oregano, basil, and shredded green and red cabbage. Simmer 10–15 minutes, covered, or until shredded cabbage is tender. Turn to lowest heat.

Add apple cider vinegar, a little at a time. The vinegar serves to mellow the taste of the tomato puree, and is especially important if using fresh tomatoes. You may need less vinegar if using canned tomato puree.

Add Bronner's seasoning and Spike, and sea salt to taste. Adjust other seasonings as desired.

You may need to add water, depending on how tightly the lid fits your soup pot. Ideally this soup should be of medium thickness, lots of cabbage with lots of thin soup broth. Adjust water as necessary; serve.

Tomato Lentil

Paul Lewin

Cooking time: 1¼ hrs.   Makes 4 qts.

A full-bodied and flavorful lentil vegetable soup. For variety, try Tomato Lentil Deluxe.

6 c. water
3 c. tomato puree—3 lg. chopped, unpeeled ripe tomatoes (or 1 1-lb. can whole or diced tomatoes and 1 c. water) blended until smooth
1 bay leaf
1½ c. (3 med.) carrots, quartered lengthwise, then diced
1½ c. (1 lg.) chopped yellow onion
2 c. (¾ lb.) lentils
2 c. (4 lg. stalks) chopped celery
2 c. (¾ lb.) diced red or green cabbage

⅓ c. diced green pepper
2 Tbsp. unrefined olive oil
1½ c. (1 med.) zucchini, sliced in ¼″ thick half-circles
3 c. (½ lb.) broccoli—thinly sliced stems; bite-sized flowerettes
2 c. tomato juice
1 tsp. granulated garlic
¾ tsp. apple cider vinegar
2–4 Tbsp. tamari, to taste
Vege-Sal or sea salt to taste

In a 5- or 6-quart pot, bring to a boil: water, tomato puree, bay leaf, carrots, onion, lentils, celery, cabbage, green pepper, and olive oil. Simmer, covered (stir occasionally), 45 minutes to 1 hour, or until lentils are very soft and all vegetables quite tender.

Add zucchini, broccoli, tomato juice, garlic, and vinegar. Simmer 10–15 minutes, or until zucchini and broccoli are tender.

Add tamari, to taste, for full-bodied flavor, and Vege-Sal or sea salt, if desired. Serve.

Variation: Tomato Lentil Deluxe

For a slightly more colorful and flavorful variation, add to the soup base $\frac{1}{4}$ bunch fresh spinach, finely chopped. Near the end, after zucchini and broccoli have cooked for a few minutes, add 1 cup fresh or frozen corn kernels and 1 cup fresh or frozen peas (if using frozen vegetables, first rinse under hot water to thaw, then steam until tender, colors bright).

Unstuffed Bell Pepper

Robin Lowe

Easy
Cooking time: 1 hr.   Makes 3–3½ qts.

This soup much resembles the flavor of a stuffed bell pepper that has indeed come unstuffed. Satisfying and flavorful.

8 c. water
¾ c. long grain brown rice
1½ c. (1 med.) diced yellow onion
2 Tbsp. olive oil
2 lg. red and 2 lg. green bell peppers—1½ c. diced; 2½ c. chopped into ¾″ squares (may use all of either red or green peppers if one is not available)
2 c. (2 lg. stalks) chopped celery

¾ c. (1 med.) diced carrot
3 cloves garlic, pressed or minced
2 tsp. crumbled oregano leaf
2 tsp. crumbled basil leaf
½ tsp. ground celery seed
1 12-oz. can tomato paste
2½ tsp. mild chili powder
3 Tbsp. tamari
Vege-Sal or sea salt to taste

In a 5- or 6-quart pot, bring to a boil: water, rice, onion, olive oil, and diced bell pepper. Reduce heat and simmer, covered, for about 25 minutes, or until rice is a little tender.

Add celery, bell pepper squares, carrot, garlic, oregano, basil, celery seed, and tomato paste. Continue simmering 20–30 minutes, or until added veggies are tender and rice is completely cooked.

Add chili powder, tamari, and Vege-Sal. Simmer 5 minutes, or until flavors are well blended. Adjust seasonings to taste. Serve.

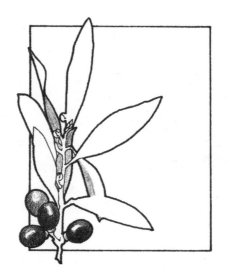